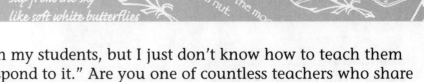

snowflakes
slip from the sky
like soft white butterflies

"I love reading poetry with my students, but I just don't know how to teach them to read a poem and respond to it." Are you one of countless teachers who share this sentiment? If so, the simple, structured lessons of *Read and Understand Poetry* are just what you need!

- Easy-to-follow lessons guide you in introducing and reading poems chosen especially for students at your grade level.

- Quick and easy minilessons help you work with your students on the language arts skills that are unique to poetry.

- Individual follow-up activity pages help students consolidate what they have learned and extend their critical thinking and creativity.

What's on the Teacher Page?

The **teacher page** provides a simple, easy-to-follow lesson plan that includes these features:

The **Before You Read** section provides important background information for you to share with students prior to reading the poem. Guidelines for developing key concepts and suggestions for preteaching vocabulary are found here.

The **While You Read** section helps you choose the best way for students to experience each poem for the first time (such as listening to you read it aloud, reading it aloud chorally or individually, reading it silently, etc.).

The **After You Read** section guides you in presenting minilessons that focus on different types of poetry and on important elements of the language arts curriculum for poetry.

What's on the Poem Page?

Each **poem page** presents:

- the text of the poetry featured in the lesson

- a simple illustration to enhance comprehension

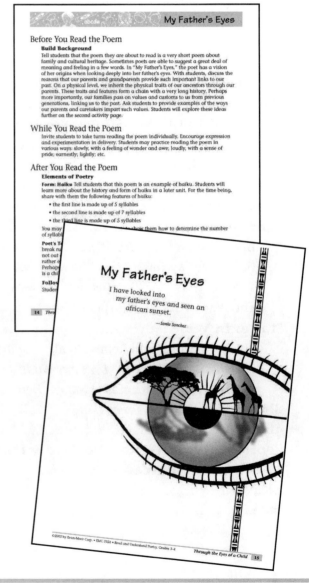

What's on the Follow-up Activity Pages?

As you guide students through the lessons outlined on the teacher page, they will have multiple opportunities to work as part of a group on developing an understanding of the form and content of each poem. The Follow-up Activities give students the opportunity to synthesize new information and practice language arts skills introduced during teacher-directed minilessons.

The first page of **Follow-up Activities** is designed to help students consolidate their comprehension of the poem by having them select the only correct response out of four possible choices for each of these multiple-choice items. Item content covers:

- literal comprehension
- sequence
- word meanings
- context clues and inferences
- main idea and details

In addition, the item format on this first activity page emulates the format students are likely to encounter on standardized language arts tests. After completing the activity pages in *Read and Understand Poetry*, students will be undaunted when a poem is presented as a reading passage on their next standardized test.

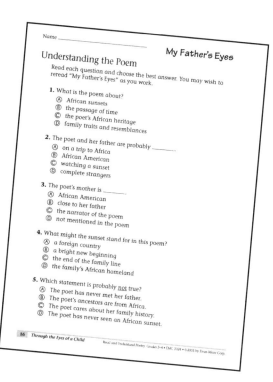

The second page of **Follow-up Activities** may focus on any aspect of the language arts curriculum touched upon in the poem. Students may be invited to share their opinions as they respond to open-ended questions, to try their hand at using poetic techniques such as onomatopoeia or alliteration, or to write a poem of their own. Critical thinking and creativity are encouraged on this type of activity page.

What Are the Additional Student Resources?

A seven-page **Glossary of Poetry Terms** features kid-friendly definitions and pronunciation guidelines for terms ranging from *alliteration* to *simile*. Each glossary entry includes an example drawn from this anthology, further strengthening students' connection to poetry terminology.

An **About the Poets** feature presents brief, high-interest information on each of the poets included in this anthology. This helps build the additional context that allows students to deepen their understanding of the work of specific poets.

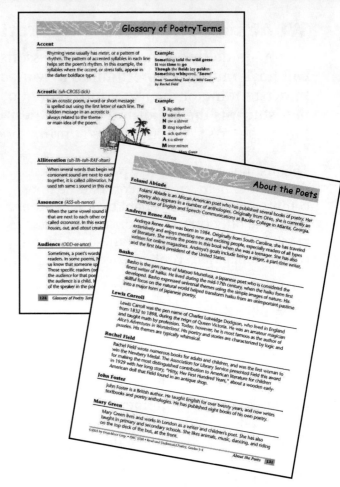

How to Use These Materials

To create a unique poetry anthology for your students, reproduce for each student:

- the cover page for the student *Read & Understand Poetry Anthology*
- the table of contents for each unit
- the poem and follow-up activity pages for each poem
- the Glossary of Poetry Terms and About the Poets pages

Place these pages together in a folder or three-ring binder to create individual poetry anthologies.

As students encounter new poems in their ongoing reading, they can use this resource to help them enjoy and deepen their knowledge of this timeless art form.

Through the Eyes of a Child

Contents

Before You Read the Poem

Build Background

Tell students that the poem they are going to read is written from the perspective of a small child. Explain: *The author of this poem is an adult, but she wrote the poem as if she were a small child. When a poet writes from a different perspective, she pretends she is somebody else. The words show what the poet thinks that person would say.* In this poem, a child tells about his or her father. Ask students why they think poets write from different perspectives. Students might say, for example, that poets take on different perspectives to learn more about other people. Share some of your own ideas as well.

While You Read the Poem

Invite students to read the poem silently to themselves. Ask students to imagine how the narrator, a small child, might sound reading the poem aloud. Then invite volunteers to give their own dramatic interpretation of the poem for the class. Encourage volunteers to take turns reading the poem aloud. Volunteers should try to use a "child's voice" in reading the poem, and they may even want to create gestures to accompany their reading.

After You Read the Poem

Elements of Poetry

Form: Stanzas Point out to students that this poem is composed of five stanzas. Explain that a stanza is a group of related sentences or phrases. In a sense, a stanza is somewhat like a paragraph. The lines in a stanza are related in the same way that the sentences of a paragraph "go together." Each stanza in this poem focuses on a particular feeling, situation, or setting. Lead a discussion about the topic of each stanza. How do the topics progress, or change? How does the last stanza "sum up" the poem?

Poet's Toolbox: Refrain Give students a simple definition of refrain, such as: *A refrain is a phrase, or set of lines, that are repeated at certain special places in a poem.* Ask students to identify the refrain in this poem ("in daddy's arms"). With students, find all the different occurrences of the refrain. Point out that the refrain gains added meaning and importance each time it is repeated. It has a soothing effect, and that is appropriate because the narrator is expressing how safe and protected he or she feels "in daddy's arms."

Follow-up Activities

Students may work independently to complete the activities on pages 8 and 9.

in daddy's arms

in daddy's arms i am tall
& close to the sun & warm
in daddy's arms

in daddy's arms
i can see over the fence out back
i can touch the bottom leaves of the big magnolia tree
in Cousin Sukie's yard
in daddy's arms

in my daddy's arms the moon is close
closer at night time when i can almost touch it
when it grins back at me from the wide twinkling skies

in daddy's arms i am tall
taller than Benny & my friends Ade & George
taller than Uncle Billy
& best of all
i am eye-ball-even-steven with my big brother Jamal

in my daddy's arms
i am strong & dark like him & laughing
happier than the circus clowns
with red painted grins
when daddy spins me round & round
& the whole world is crazy upside down
i am big and strong & proud like him
in daddy's arms
my daddy

—Folami Abiade

Name _____

Understanding the Poem

Read each question and choose the best answer. You may wish to reread "in daddy's arms" as you work.

1. Jamal is the narrator's _____.

   Ⓐ big brother

   Ⓑ best friend

   Ⓒ cousin

   Ⓓ uncle

2. At the end of the poem, the narrator _____.

   Ⓐ dresses up like a clown

   Ⓑ spins around in daddy's arms

   Ⓒ grows up to be just like daddy

   Ⓓ imagines what it's like to be big and strong

3. The phrase "eye-ball-even-steven" probably means _____.

   Ⓐ close enough to see

   Ⓑ at the same level

   Ⓒ taller than

   Ⓓ best of all

4. The poem tells _____.

   Ⓐ how badly the narrator wants to be like his or her father

   Ⓑ how the narrator feels when with his or her father

   Ⓒ why children should respect their parents

   Ⓓ what it's like to be a child

5. You can tell that the narrator's family probably _____.

   Ⓐ is funny and goofy

   Ⓑ moves around a lot

   Ⓒ is scattered far and wide

   Ⓓ spends a lot of time together

Understanding the Poem

First, read the lines from the poem. Then show what they mean by completing each sentence.

1. *in daddy's arms i am tall*
   & close to the sun & warm
   in daddy's arms

The narrator's father makes her feel _____.

2. *in daddy's arms*
   i can see over the fence out back
   i can touch the bottom leaves of the big magnolia tree

The narrator feels taller than she really is because her father

_____

_____.

3. *in my daddy's arms the moon is close*
   closer at night time when i can almost touch it
   when it grins back at me from the wide twinkling skies

You can tell that the narrator is happy because _____

_____.

4. *in daddy's arms i am tall*
   taller than Benny & my friends Ade & George

The narrator must be a child because _____

_____.

5. *when daddy spins me round & round*
   & the whole world is crazy upside down
   i am big and strong & proud like him

The narrator's father must be a good parent because _____

_____.

Before You Read the Poem

Build Background

Ask students what they think this poem will be about, based on the title. If necessary, ask questions such as: *Do you think the poem is about the color black? What else do we mean when we use the word* black? Confirm for students that *black* is commonly used in our society when talking about African Americans. Strictly speaking, it refers to skin color, although it is also used when talking about African American heritage and black culture. Ask students if they think the author of this poem is black, and why they think so. It is very probable that students will know in advance that the author is black, and that the poem is about black pride. Ask students to keep this in mind while reading the poem. You might tell them now or after they read the poem that poet Andreya Renee Allen wrote "Black Is Beautiful" when she was a teenager.

While You Read the Poem

Ask several volunteers to demonstrate how they think the poem should be read. The poem invites a rhythmic, almost rap-like reading. Ask one of the volunteers to lead the class in a choral reading of the poem. Conduct this choral reading several times until students are familiar with the poem. Challenge students to read the poem aloud without looking at the text.

After You Read the Poem

Elements of Poetry

Form: Free Verse Tell students that this poem is written as free verse. That means that it does not use any special pattern of rhyme, or meter. Invite students to find the places in the poem where there are natural pauses. Although all students may not "hear" pauses in the same places, they should all notice that it sounds awkward and choppy to pause at the end of every line.

Poet's Toolbox: Italics and Boldface Explain to students that italics and boldface are "typesetting tools" poets can use to emphasize words to make them stand out. Point out the use of italics in the third line: "Black is *the* color." Explain that italicized words are read with emphasis. The poet also put certain words in boldface type to make those words stand out. The boldfaced words are also set in a larger size than the rest of the words in the poem. The poet may or may not have intended for the boldfaced words to be read with emphasis or greater volume. It could be that she simply wanted the printed page to have a dynamic, active look that fit the poem. Ask students why they think the poet used boldface in the way she did.

Follow-up Activities

Students may work independently to complete the activities on pages 12 and 13.

Read and Understand Poetry • EMC 3324 • ©2005 by Evan-Moor Corp.

Black Is Beautiful

Black is beautiful
Black is me
Black is *the* color
    can't you see
    that

blue **is** nice,
and orange is neat
but they can't compete
    because

Black is beautiful
Black is me
Tall, dark, and wonderful
    see!

—*Andreya Renee Allen*

Understanding the Poem

Read each question and choose the best answer. You may wish to reread "Black Is Beautiful" as you work.

1. In this poem, the poet is talking about _____.

Ⓐ the differences between colors

Ⓑ all the meanings of the word *black*

Ⓒ some colors of the rainbow

Ⓓ skin color

2. You can tell that the poet _____.

Ⓐ is black

Ⓑ can't see

Ⓒ is white but wants to be black

Ⓓ thinks she is better than everybody else

3. What does the poet mean when she says that blue and orange "can't compete"?

Ⓐ They are "loser" colors.

Ⓑ They don't look good together.

Ⓒ They aren't as beautiful as black.

Ⓓ They look as good as any other color.

4. How does the poet feel about her color?

Ⓐ proud

Ⓑ meek

Ⓒ unconcerned

Ⓓ too good for words

5. Which statement would the poet probably agree with?

Ⓐ People are all the same.

Ⓑ Be proud of who you are.

Ⓒ Different colors don't mix.

Ⓓ Don't pay attention to skin color.

Read and Understand Poetry • EMC 3324 • ©2005 by Evan-Moor Corp.

Black Is Beautiful

Understanding the Poem

1. List some of the words that the poet uses to describe herself.

_____

_____

2. The author of this poem is black, or African American. What do you know about your racial and cultural background? Write a few lines that tell about your family history and where your ancestors came from.

_____

_____

_____

3. What is your cultural identity? Are you American? Are you connected to more than one culture? Write a few sentences or a list of words that tell how you feel about your culture or what you think about it.

_____

_____

_____

_____

4. Do you think it's important to know about your race? Why or why not? Explain your answer.

_____

_____

_____

_____

Before You Read the Poem

Build Background

Tell students that the poem they are about to read is a very short poem about family and cultural heritage. Sometimes poets are able to suggest a great deal of meaning and feeling in a few words. In "My Father's Eyes," the poet has a vision of her origins when looking deeply into her father's eyes. With students, discuss the reasons that our parents and grandparents provide such important links to our past. On a physical level, we inherit the physical traits of our ancestors through our parents. These traits and features form a chain with a very long history. Perhaps more importantly, our families pass on values and customs to us from previous generations, linking us to the past. Ask students to provide examples of the ways our parents and caretakers impart such values. Students will explore these ideas further on the second activity page.

While You Read the Poem

Invite students to take turns reading the poem individually. Encourage expression and experimentation in delivery. Students may practice reading the poem in various ways: slowly, with a feeling of wonder and awe; loudly, with a sense of pride; earnestly; lightly; etc.

After You Read the Poem

Elements of Poetry

Form: Haiku Tell students that this poem is an example of haiku. Students will learn more about the history and form of haiku in a later unit. For the time being, share with them the following features of haiku:

- the first line is made up of 5 syllables

- the second line is made up of 7 syllables

- the third line is made up of 5 syllables

You may wish to work with students to show them how to determine the number of syllables in each line.

Poet's Toolbox: Capitalization Poets often use fanciful spellings and purposely break rules of capitalization and punctuation. They do this for an intended effect—not out of laziness! Students should be able to find the "violation" in this poem rather easily. The poet neglected to capitalize the word *african* in the third line. Perhaps the poet did this to help suggest that the narrator, or speaker, in the poem is a child.

Follow-up Activities

Students may work independently to complete the activities on pages 16 and 17.

Read and Understand Poetry • EMC 3324 • ©2005 by Evan-Moor Corp.

My Father's Eyes

I have looked into
  my father's eyes and seen an
  african sunset.

—*Sonia Sanchez*

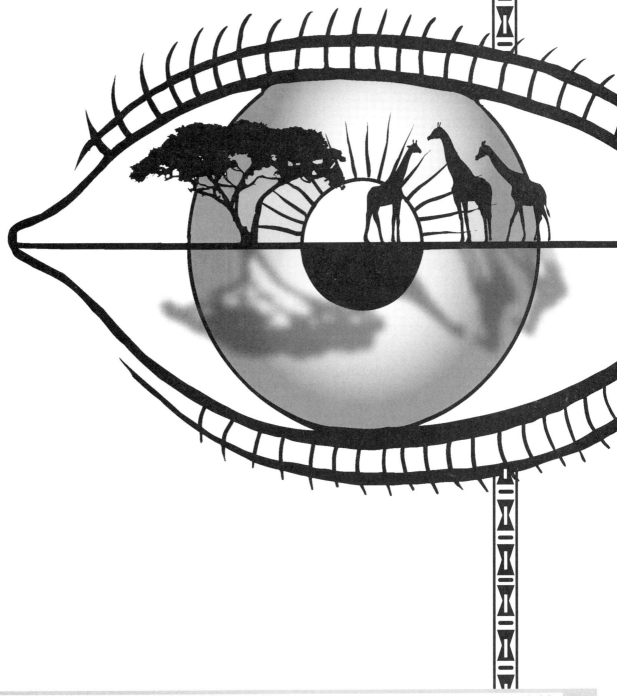

My Father's Eyes

Understanding the Poem

Read each question and choose the best answer. You may wish to reread "My Father's Eyes" as you work.

1. What is the poem about?
- Ⓐ African sunsets
- Ⓑ the passage of time
- Ⓒ the poet's African heritage
- Ⓓ family traits and resemblances

2. The poet and her father are probably _____.
- Ⓐ on a trip to Africa
- Ⓑ African American
- Ⓒ watching a sunset
- Ⓓ complete strangers

3. The poet's mother is _____.
- Ⓐ African American
- Ⓑ close to her father
- Ⓒ the narrator of the poem
- Ⓓ not mentioned in the poem

4. What might the sunset stand for in this poem?
- Ⓐ a foreign country
- Ⓑ a bright new beginning
- Ⓒ the end of the family line
- Ⓓ the family's African homeland

5. Which statement is probably <u>not</u> true?
- Ⓐ The poet has never met her father.
- Ⓑ The poet's ancestors are from Africa.
- Ⓒ The poet cares about her family history.
- Ⓓ The poet has never seen an African sunset.

Understanding the Poem

1. Where are the poet's ancestors from? How do you know?

_____

_____ .

2. Where are your ancestors from?

_____

_____ .

3. What else do you know about your ancestors?

_____

_____ .

4. What are some of the things that connect you to the family members who lived before you? Think about your physical traits, culture, and values.

_____

_____

_____

5. What are some of the ways we pass our culture on from one generation to the next?

_____

_____

_____

_____ .

Before You Read the Poem

Build Background

Ask students if they have ever been so sick that they had to stay in bed for several days or more. People who have spent long periods of time in bed often say that the biggest challenge of a lengthy illness is finding ways to stay entertained. Ask students to share about the games and pastimes that could help make time go by during such an illness. Introduce the poem by saying that "The Land of Counterpane" is about a boy who uses his imagination to create a whole world while he's sick in bed.

Build Vocabulary

This poem was written more than one hundred years ago, and it contains words and phrases that have fallen out of use. Other phrases that may sound "old-fashioned" are simply fanciful expressions created by the poet himself. Explain the following words:

a-bed: in bed

bed-clothes: sheets and blankets

dale: a valley

counterpane: a bedspread

While You Read the Poem

Model how to read the poem aloud, encouraging students to chime in with you. When students have familiarized themselves with the poem, form four groups of students. Assign one of the poem's four stanzas to each group. Ask the first group to study the first stanza for a minute and then challenge them to recite the stanza aloud without looking at the page. Continue in this way until the other three groups have recited their assigned stanzas as well.

After You Read the Poem

Elements of Poetry

Form: Rhyming Verse Point out the rhyming pair *a-bed* and *head* in the first stanza. Tell students that poets usually establish a rhyming pattern in the first stanza and then stick to that pattern throughout the poem. The rhyming pattern of the first stanza of this poem could be represented as *aabb*. Ask students to confirm that this pattern is followed throughout the poem.

Poet's Toolbox: Assonance Tell students that assonance is the repetition of a vowel sound within a short phrase. As an example, point out the phrase "houses out" at the end of the third line in the third stanza. Having the *ou* sound in both words makes the phrase fun to read and easy to remember. Ask students to help you find other examples of assonance in the poem. Make sure that they include "pillow-hill" and "dale and plain" in the last stanza. Students will have more practice with assonance on the second activity page.

Follow-up Activities

Students may work independently to complete the activities on pages 20 and 21.

Read and Understand Poetry • EMC 3324 • ©2005 by Evan-Moor Corp.

The Land of Counterpane

When I was sick and lay a-bed,
I had two pillows at my head,
And all my toys beside me lay
To keep me happy all the day.

And sometimes for an hour or so
I watched my leaden soldiers go,
With different uniforms and drills,
Among the bed-clothes, through the hills;

And sometimes sent my ships in fleets
All up and down among the sheets;
Or brought my trees and houses out,
And planted cities all about.

I was the giant great and still
That sits upon the pillow-hill,
And sees before him, dale and plain,
The pleasant land of counterpane.

—*Robert Louis Stevenson*

 Did You Know? Robert Louis Stevenson was often sick in bed for long periods of time, just like the boy in "The Land of Counterpane." To pass the time, he created fanciful poems and stories. Some of his stories—*Kidnapped* and *Treasure Island*, to name just a few—are now classics.

Understanding the Poem

Read each question and choose the best answer. You may wish to reread "The Land of Counterpane" as you work.

1. Where does this poem take place?
   - Ⓐ on a bed
   - Ⓑ in a castle
   - Ⓒ in a toy chest
   - Ⓓ on the high seas

2. The narrator of the poem is _____.
   - Ⓐ lazy
   - Ⓑ sick
   - Ⓒ lost
   - Ⓓ asleep

3. You can tell the narrator of the poem is _____.
   - Ⓐ a child waking up from a dream
   - Ⓑ a nurse taking care of a sick boy
   - Ⓒ a boy pretending to be grown up
   - Ⓓ an adult looking back on his childhood

4. In the poem, the phrase "lay a-bed" means _____.
   - Ⓐ stayed in bed
   - Ⓑ made the bed
   - Ⓒ laid a bed down
   - Ⓓ messed up the sheets

5. What is "The Land of Counterpane"?
   - Ⓐ a dream
   - Ⓑ a kingdom by the sea
   - Ⓒ a make-believe world
   - Ⓓ a picture on a windowpane

Read and Understand Poetry • EMC 3324 • ©2005 by Evan-Moor Corp.

Understanding the Poem

1. The narrator of "The Land of Counterpane" pretends that certain things in his bedroom are larger than life. Tell how the boy sees these things in his imagination.

He pretends that his pillows _____.

His sheets look like _____.

His bedspread, or counterpane, turns into _____

_____.

2. Read this list of everyday things. What could each of these things look like with a little imagination?

rug _____

mirror _____

fireplace _____

sink _____

salt and pepper shakers _____

3. *Assonance* is the repetition of vowel sounds. You can hear it in phrases such as *pillow-hill* and *dale and plain*. For each of the words below, write another word with the same vowel sound. Then read your assonant words to a partner.

fleet   _____

head   _____

out   _____

day   _____

go   _____

Nature's Mysteries

Contents

Read and Understand Poetry • EMC 3324 • ©2005 by Evan-Moor Corp.

Before You Read the Poem

Build Background

Nature poems often explore the wonder and mystery of the natural world. Poets love to pose questions about nature that can't really be answered in a logical way. Poets and children alike are famous for asking questions such as, "Where does the wind come from?" With students, brainstorm a list of "impossible questions" that they would like to ask Mother Nature, if they could. On the board, write the prompt *I wish I knew _____*. Ask students to help you complete the prompt, writing sentences such as *I wish I knew why the seasons change*, and *I wish I knew where the sun goes in winter*. Have students compare these rhetorical questions to those in the poem "I Wish I Knew."

While You Read the Poem

Form two groups of students. Have each group read aloud one of the stanzas in the poem. When they are finished, ask each group to practice reading the other stanza. Challenge groups to memorize their assigned stanza by looking at the poem for 30 seconds (or so) and then saying the poem aloud without looking at the printed page.

After You Read the Poem

Elements of Poetry

Form: Lyric Share with students these contrasting definitions: *Narrative poetry tells a story. Lyric poetry shares feelings and impressions.* Ask students whether "I Wish I Knew" is a narrative poem or a lyric poem, and to explain why. Confirm for them that it is a lyric poem because it conveys the poet's thoughts and impressions, or musings, on the mystery and essence of winter.

Poet's Toolbox: Homophones Explain to students that homophones are pairs of words that sound the same, even though they are spelled differently. Examples of homophones are *sun* and *son*; *threw* and *through*; *see* and *sea*. Poets use homophones to create rhyming pairs, although this is a technique that poets are advised against overusing. More pleasing rhymes are those that are almost, but not exactly, the same. Ask students to find the pair of homophones in this poem (*new* and *knew*).

Follow-up Activities

Students may work independently to complete the activities on pages 25 and 26.

I Wish I Knew

Winter,
I wish I knew
The way you make
Each snowflake new,
Just how you think up
Each design—

Winter,
I wish I knew
The secret of your mind.

—*Beverly McLoughland*

Understanding the Poem

Read each question and choose the best answer. You may wish to reread "I Wish I Knew" as you work.

1. This poem is about _____.
- Ⓐ water and snow
- Ⓑ a wish that came true
- Ⓒ a magical time of day
- Ⓓ one of the four seasons

2. The poet wants to know _____.
- Ⓐ the right way to make a wish
- Ⓑ how to communicate with nature
- Ⓒ why each snowflake is so unique
- Ⓓ how one season changes into another

3. The speaker of the poem _____.
- Ⓐ is a human being
- Ⓑ is a force of nature
- Ⓒ knows all the secrets of nature
- Ⓓ makes a special design for every snowflake

4. The poem is addressed to _____.
- Ⓐ winter
- Ⓑ the poet
- Ⓒ the reader
- Ⓓ a snowflake

5. According to this poem, nature is _____.
- Ⓐ perfect the way it is
- Ⓑ beautiful in its simplicity
- Ⓒ complicated and highly technical
- Ⓓ impossible to understand completely

Name _____

Understanding the Poem

The author of this poem personifies winter. That is, she speaks about winter as if it were a human being. She says that Winter "thinks up designs for snowflakes." What would you add to that? How could you personify the other seasons? Add more examples.

Winter

Winter paints the world white.

_____
_____
_____
_____
_____
_____
_____

Spring

Spring invites the birds to sing.

_____
_____
_____
_____
_____
_____
_____

Summer

_____
_____
_____
_____
_____
_____
_____

Fall

_____
_____
_____
_____
_____
_____
_____

Before You Read the Poem

Build Background

With students, conduct a discussion about the properties and characteristics of the wind. Ask: *What color is the wind? What shape is it? Can you put the wind in a box? Why not?* In this way, guide students to the conclusion that the wind is shapeless, invisible, and very changeable. Tell students that the poem they are about to read is a lighthearted celebration of the wind's mysterious nature.

While You Read the Poem

Form two groups of students. Have each group read alternate lines of the poem in a chantlike manner. If necessary, model an appropriate rhythm by clapping your hands. Then have groups switch and practice reading the other set of lines.

After You Read the Poem

Elements of Poetry

Form: Chant This poem is written as a chant. Chants are simple, repetitive rhymes that are meant to be read aloud in a way that accentuates their inherent rhythm. A chant is often based on a traditional song or melody, but it may also be based on an invented melody. Readers can discover the melody by experimenting while they read the chant aloud. Poets such as Pat Mora often choose to create their own chants by using short, repetitive phrases with variable elements. With students, identify the repetitive elements of this poem and the prepositional phrase that varies from line to line: "in the morning," "in my two hands," etc. Point out that the final line also contains a combination of repetition and variation: "run and spin," "dance and spin," "run and spin."

Poet's Toolbox: Rhetorical Questions "Can I, Can I Catch the Wind" consists of a series of rhetorical questions. Ask students what the answer to each of these questions is. They will undoubtedly reply that the answer to each question is "no." Tell students that such questions are rhetorical. The poet asks them, even though the answer is obvious, to guide the reader toward an appreciation of the wind's invisible, shapeless nature.

Follow-up Activities

Students may work independently to complete the activities on pages 29 and 30.

Can I, Can I Catch the Wind

Can I, can I catch the wind, in the morning, catch the wind?
Can I, can I catch the wind, in my two hands, catch the wind?
Can I, can I catch the wind, in my basket, catch the wind?
Can I, can I catch the wind, in my clay pot, catch the wind?
Can I, can I catch the wind, in my tin box, catch the wind?
Can I, can I catch the wind, in my straw hat, catch the wind?
Can I, can I catch the wind, in my bird cage, catch the wind?
Wind, Wind, run and spin, dance and spin, run and spin.

—*Pat Mora*

Read and Understand Poetry • EMC 3324 • ©2005 by Evan-Moor Corp.

Understanding the Poem

Read each question and choose the best answer. You may wish to reread "Can I, Can I Catch the Wind" as you work.

1. This poem is written _____.
- Ⓐ to a friend
- Ⓑ as a riddle
- Ⓒ as a list of questions
- Ⓓ with hardly any repetition

2. In this poem, the poet _____.
- Ⓐ asks questions that are impossible to answer
- Ⓑ asks questions that have obvious answers
- Ⓒ makes one joke after another
- Ⓓ makes false statements

3. Which of the following things does the poet not use to try to catch the wind?
- Ⓐ a clay pot
- Ⓑ a straw hat
- Ⓒ a fishing net
- Ⓓ her own two hands

4. The poet probably wrote this poem to _____ the reader.
- Ⓐ trick
- Ⓑ inform
- Ⓒ persuade
- Ⓓ entertain

5. Which statement best summarizes the meaning of the poem?
- Ⓐ The wind can't be seen or held.
- Ⓑ You have to be very clever to catch the wind.
- Ⓒ Nobody knows where the wind comes from.
- Ⓓ Some things are better than others for catching the wind.

Understanding the Poem

1. The poet asks a lot of rhetorical questions in this poem. What is a rhetorical question?

_____

_____

2. What are the answers to the questions in this poem? Explain why the questions must be answered in this way.

_____

_____

3. Why do you think the poet uses rhetorical questions in this poem?

_____

_____

4. Create a rhetorical question for each of the following elements of nature:

a. sunbeam: _____ ?

b. star: _____ ?

c. lightning bolt: _____ ?

d. night: _____ ?

e. water: _____ ?

f. sand: _____ ?

5. On a separate sheet of paper, use one of the rhetorical questions you wrote to create your own poem. Use "Can I, Can I Catch the Wind" as a model.

Read and Understand Poetry • EMC 3324 • ©2005 by Evan-Moor Corp.

Before You Read the Poem

Build Background

Tell students that they are going to read a nature poem. In this kind of poem, an aspect of nature is contemplated, or thought deeply about. Sometimes, the poet may ask a question about nature as a starting point. In this poem, poet Christina Rossetti asks, "Who Has Seen the Wind?" With students, hold a minidebate on whether or not the wind can be "seen." Some students may point out that the wind is a movement of air—because air is invisible, the wind can't be seen. Others may argue that rising dust, swaying trees, and other effects of the wind allow us to "see" it. Introduce the poem by saying, *Let's see what the poet has to say about it.*

While You Read the Poem

Invite students to take turns reading the poem aloud for the class. As they read, classmates may softly whistle, rustle paper, and create other sound effects to mimic the sound of the wind. The reader may also want to emphasize the whistling sound of the words *who*, *when*, and *wind* to add to the effect.

After You Read the Poem

Elements of Poetry

Poet's Toolbox: Repetition The poet cleverly uses repetition of form and vocabulary to create a melody that is reminiscent of a lullaby. The question "Who has seen the wind?" is repeated in the first line of both stanzas. In the first stanza, the response is "Neither I nor you," but in the second stanza it is "Neither you nor I." The slight variation in syntax prevents the pattern from becoming overly repetitive and boring; it also allows for a new rhyme in the last line of each stanza. The last two lines of each stanza begin with "But," signifying that the poet is going to modify her initial answer to the question. Guide students in discovering these structural elements by asking them to make their own observations about the similarities and differences in each stanza.

Poet's Toolbox: Personification Define the term *personification* for students, explaining that this technique allows poets to describe things, ideas, or natural forces as if they were human beings. In this poem, Rossetti describes the wind and trees as if they were living, breathing beings. How does she do this? Ask students to look for examples in the text. The poet says, for example, that the leaves in the tree are "trembling," as if the tree were anticipating the approaching wind. In the second stanza, the trees "bow down their heads," showing their respect for the wind. The total effect is to make the wind appear magical, mysterious, and powerful.

Follow-up Activities

Students may work independently to complete the activities on pages 33 and 34.

Who Has Seen the Wind?

Who has seen the wind?
2 Neither I nor you:
But when the leaves hang trembling
4 The wind is passing thro'.

Who has seen the wind?
6 Neither you nor I:
But when the trees bow down their heads
8 The wind is passing by.

—*Christina Rossetti*

Did You Know? Christina Rossetti was born in London in 1830. Her brother was a painter, and sometimes he painted pictures of her. They both submitted work to a magazine called *Germ.* Christina wrote many poems, especially for children and young adults.

Read and Understand Poetry • EMC 3324 • ©2005 by Evan-Moor Corp.

Understanding the Poem

Read each question and choose the best answer. You may wish to reread "Who Has Seen the Wind?" as you work.

1. In this poem, the wind is _____.
- (A) everywhere and nowhere at the same time
- (B) powerful and mysterious
- (C) violent and destructive
- (D) seen but not felt

2. In line 4, *thro'* is an abbreviation for _____.
- (A) throw
- (B) threw
- (C) through
- (D) thorough

3. What does "Neither you nor I" mean?
- (A) either one of us
- (B) both of us
- (C) you, but not I
- (D) not you and not I

4. Which of these is the answer to the question in the title?
- (A) Only trees can "see" the wind.
- (B) You can't see the wind, but you can feel its presence.
- (C) Anybody can see the wind if they look hard enough.
- (D) Only poets and people who read their poems see the wind.

5. The author of this poem probably _____.
- (A) can't stand to go outside
- (B) has lived through a hurricane
- (C) has a deep appreciation for nature
- (D) believes only in things that she can see

Name _____

Understanding the Poem

Try writing your own nature poem. Follow the same rhyming pattern
and meter as "Who Has Seen the Wind?" Study the example, and then
fill in the blank spaces. When you are finished, write your poem on a
separate sheet of paper. Choose one of these titles, or create your own:
"Who Has Touched a Star?"; "Who Has Heard an Ant?"; "Who Has
Kissed a Cloud?"

Who has seen the wind?	(5 syllables)
Neither I nor you:	(5 syllables)
But when the leaves hang trembling	(7 syllables)
The wind is passing thro'.	(6 syllables)
Who has seen the wind?	(5 syllables)
Neither you nor I:	(5 syllables)
But when the trees bow down their heads	(8 syllables)
The wind is passing by.	(6 syllables)

Who has _____ ?

Neither I nor you:

But when _____

_____ .

(Last word must rhyme with *you*.)

Who has _____ ?

Neither you nor I:

But when _____

_____ .

(Last word must rhyme with *I*.)

 Read and Understand Poetry • EMC 3324 • ©2005 by Evan-Moor Corp.

Before You Read the Poem

Build Background

Talk with students about caterpillars and the process called *metamorphosis*. A caterpillar is a wormlike creature that eventually metamorphoses, or develops, into a butterfly or moth. The process usually only takes a few weeks, but in very cold climates it can take two to three years. Butterflies and moths are closely related insects, but there are a few important differences. One of these differences is that butterflies migrate during the day, and moths fly only at night. This poem is about a "race" between a butterfly and a moth as they migrate through several seasons. It is loosely based on biological facts, but it definitely shouldn't be regarded as a science lesson!

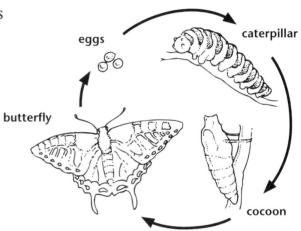

While You Read the Poem

Ask for five volunteers to read the poem aloud for the class. Have each volunteer read one of the five stanzas of the poem. When they are finished, ask for five more volunteers. Repeat as necessary so that all students have an opportunity to read for the class.

After You Read the Poem

Elements of Poetry

Form: Narrative Verse This poem is a narrative—it tells a story. As such, it has characters, a setting, and a sequence of events. Ask students to identify these elements in the poem. You may want to record their suggestions in the form of a story map. Events may be plotted in two parallel lines, showing the efforts of the butterfly and moth to beat each other in their "race."

Poet's Toolbox: Comparisons In this poem, the poet uses quite a few contrasts and comparisons. Not only does he contrast the butterfly and moth, but there are also comparisons between the different seasons, day and night, rates of speed, and distances traveled. Contrasts help to define scenery and characters; it is easier to "see" something when it is compared to something else. Ask students to identify and explain the different contrasts and comparisons that are presented in the poem.

Follow-up Activities

Students may work independently to complete the activities on pages 37 and 38.

Caterpillar Race

Two little caterpillars had a race
down the middle of a long dirt trail.
One was as fast as molasses.
The other was as quick as a snail.

They started out in early morning—
moved a quarter inch by noon.
By the time they'd gotten twenty feet
they'd turned into cocoons.

Winter passed and then came spring.
They both emerged in May.
One was a butterfly, the other a moth,
and they flew the rest of the way.

One traveled by day, the other by night
to get where they were going.
Five months later, they called "time out"
when they realized it was snowing!

They met again in the spring
when the cold went by.
They each agreed they <u>both</u> were fast
and called the race a tie.

—*John Himmelman*

Read and Understand Poetry • EMC 3324 • ©2005 by Evan-Moor Corp.

Name _____

Understanding the Poem

Read each question and choose the best answer. You may wish to reread "Caterpillar Race" as you work.

1. What is this poem about?
    Ⓐ the life of a caterpillar
    Ⓑ the changing seasons
    Ⓒ a meeting between two caterpillars
    Ⓓ a race between a butterfly and a moth

2. The two caterpillars turned into _____ .
    Ⓐ snails
    Ⓑ moths
    Ⓒ cocoons
    Ⓓ butterflies

3. When the poet says that one is "as fast as molasses," he means that it's _____ .
    Ⓐ sticky
    Ⓑ very fast
    Ⓒ very slow
    Ⓓ like liquid

4. How much time passes in this poem?
    Ⓐ almost two years
    Ⓑ less than a year
    Ⓒ two seasons
    Ⓓ five months

5. Which statement best describes this poem?
    Ⓐ It could actually happen.
    Ⓑ It's based on a true story.
    Ⓒ It has nothing to do with reality.
    Ⓓ It is partly based on facts but is mostly made up.

Caterpillar Race

Understanding the Poem

1. There are many ways to compare two things. One way is to use the word *as* in a sentence, such as *It was <u>as</u> cold <u>as</u> ice.* Find two comparisons in the poem that use *as*. Write them here.

_____

_____

2. List two animals or things from nature that could "compete" in a race or some other competition.

_____   _____

3. Write one or two sentences to compare the two things you chose above. Use *as* in your comparison.

_____

_____

4. Write a paragraph about their competition. Be sure to use the comparisons you wrote above.

_____

_____

_____

_____

_____

_____

_____

_____

    Read and Understand Poetry • EMC 3324 • ©2005 by Evan-Moor Corp.

Before You Read the Poem

Build Background

The following poem paints a picture of a New England landscape in the wintertime. Point out New England on a U.S. map, including the states of Maine, Vermont, New Hampshire, and Massachusetts. If possible, show students pictures of a winter scene in New England. Ask students to describe or imagine such a scene. *How does snow change the landscape? What does it look like as it falls, and what sound does it make?*

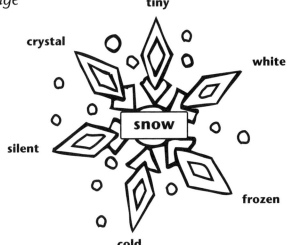

Build Vocabulary

Ask students to suggest words that describe the way snow sounds, looks, and feels. Record their suggestions in a simple graphic organizer. Ask students to refer to the graphic organizer as they read the poem. Do they see any of their ideas represented in the poem?

While You Read the Poem

Lead the class in a choral recitation of the poem. After reading the poem two or three times chorally, invite a volunteer to read it aloud for the class. Students may enjoy hearing the poem read aloud several times by different readers. Encourage all students who wish to try reading it aloud.

After You Read the Poem

Elements of Poetry

Form: Rhyming Verse Point out to students that this is a rhyming poem. The final word in each line rhymes with the final word in another line. Ask students to help you identify the rhyming pattern, which is *ababcc.*

Poet's Toolbox: Alliteration Tell students that alliteration is the repetition of an initial vowel or consonant in a pair or string of words. Examples of alliteration include a "**s**erious **s**ea **s**torm" and "the **m**ysterious, **m**agical **m**oon." Alliteration is a common technique in poetry and other fanciful forms of language, including advertisements, because such expressions are easy to remember. Ask students to find the two examples of alliteration in "Snow-Flakes": "brown and bare" and "Silent, and soft, and slow." Students will do further work with alliteration on the second activity page.

Follow-up Activities

Students may work independently to complete the activities on pages 41 and 42.

Snow-Flakes

Out of the bosom of the Air,
Out of the cloud-folds of her garments shaken,
Over the woodlands brown and bare,
Over the harvest-fields forsaken,
Silent, and soft, and slow
Descends the snow.

—*Henry Wadsworth Longfellow*

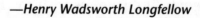

Did You Know? Henry Wadsworth Longfellow was born in an old wooden house by the seaside in Portland, Maine, in 1807. He studied law for a while, but in the end, he decided to follow his heart and become a poet. His poems are about the people and landscape of America in the 1800s.

Understanding the Poem

Read each question and choose the best answer. You may wish to reread "Snow-Flakes" as you work.

1. The setting of this poem is _____.
   Ⓐ a frozen lake
   Ⓑ a stormy sea
   Ⓒ a field in the winter
   Ⓓ a mountaintop in the springtime

2. The snowflake travels _____.
   Ⓐ from cloud to cloud
   Ⓑ all day and into the night
   Ⓒ down from the sky before it melts
   Ⓓ over the woods and then over a field

3. Which of these is another phrase that means "the bosom of the Air"?
   Ⓐ empty space
   Ⓑ high in the sky
   Ⓒ here and there
   Ⓓ close to the ground

4. The poet compares the clouds to _____.
   Ⓐ a farm
   Ⓑ a woodland
   Ⓒ a fancy hairstyle
   Ⓓ a dress with folds

5. Which of these means about the same as *forsaken*?
   Ⓐ frozen
   Ⓑ ripened
   Ⓒ abandoned
   Ⓓ overcrowded

Name _____

Understanding the Poem

Alliteration is the repetition of the same sound at the beginning of two or more words that are close together. In the phrase *magical moon,* for example, both words start with the letter *m.* Use what you know about alliteration to complete these activities.

1. Circle the alliteration in this line from the poem:

"**Over the woodlands brown and bare,**"

2. Circle the letter that makes the alliteration in these lines:

"**Silent, and soft, and slow**

Descends the snow."

3. Write a word in each of the blank spaces to make the words alliterate.

   a. _____ grass grows in the grove.

   b. The _____ trees twist and turn in the tornado.

   c. A _____ butterfly brushed by me.

   d. She sells _____ by the seashore.

4. Now, you try to create alliteration. Make phrases or whole sentences using these words from the poem.

   a. clouds: _____

   b. woodlands: _____

   c. fields: _____

   d. snow: _____

Read and Understand Poetry • EMC 3324 • ©2005 by Evan-Moor Corp.

Before You Read the Poem

Build Background

Tell students that the poem they are about to read is about the migration of wild geese. Ask students what they know about bird migration. They will likely know that migratory birds travel north in the spring and south in the fall, but it may surprise them to find out the distances that some geese travel. The snow goose, for example, spends the winter in the coastal marshes of Louisiana and Texas. In the early spring, it migrates all the way to the arctic tundra. Migrating geese are guided by landmarks on the Earth's surface, the stars, prevailing winds, and scent.

While You Read the Poem

Model how to read the poem for students. Pay close attention to the poem's meter; you will find the accented syllables naturally. After the first reading, have students echo you line by line. Listen and help students find the intended stress patterns. Students may take turns reading the poem aloud for the class.

After You Read the Poem

Elements of Poetry

Poet's Toolbox: Accent/Stress Explain to students that rhyming verse has meter, which is the pattern of rhythm in the poem. One element that helps set the rhythm of the poem is the pattern of accented syllables in each line. Ask students to say the word *poetry* aloud and notice where the accent, or stress, falls (on the first syllable: **po**-e-try). Work with students to identify the accented syllables (or words) in a line from the poem, such as **Some**-thing **whis**-pered, "**Snow**!" Students may need to clap or tap a beat to help them feel the stress on these syllables. Assign other lines from the poem to partners and ask them to identify the accented syllables. Have partners share their findings with the group. There may be differences in the way students interpret stress patterns. As long as their approach works in their recitation, acknowledge that various interpretations are possible. Students will have more practice identifying accented syllables on the second activity page.

Poet's Toolbox: Consonance Students have already been introduced to the concept of assonance: the repetition of vowel sounds. Introduce students to *consonance*, explaining that it is the repetition of a final consonant sound, as in *first* and *last*. Help students discover the poet's use of consonance in "Something Told the Wild Geese." Explain that consonance can sometimes be established by stringing words with the same final consonant sound throughout the poem. In this poem, the poet has included a number of words that end in -*ing*: *something* (four times), *stirring*, and *sagging*. These words do not occupy rhyming positions, but the repetition of the -*ing* sound at key points has a musical effect, which is why poets use this technique.

Follow-up Activities

Students may work independently to complete the activities on pages 45 and 46.

Something Told the Wild Geese

Something told the wild geese
It was time to go,
Though the fields lay golden
Something whispered, "Snow!"

Leaves were green and stirring,
Berries lustre-glossed,
But beneath warm feathers
Something cautioned, "Frost!"

All the sagging orchards
Steamed with amber spice,
But each wild beast stiffened
At remembered ice.

Something told the wild geese
It was time to fly—
Summer sun was on their wings,
Winter in their cry.

—Rachel Field

Understanding the Poem

Read each question and choose the best answer. You may wish to reread "Something Told the Wild Geese" as you work.

1. What time of year is it in this poem?

Ⓐ fall

Ⓑ spring

Ⓒ winter

Ⓓ summer

2. Which of the following is mentioned in the poem?

Ⓐ Snow is falling.

Ⓑ The fields are golden.

Ⓒ Flowers are coming out.

Ⓓ Birds are making their nests.

3. At the end of the first stanza, what does the word *cautioned* mean?

Ⓐ warned

Ⓑ stopped

Ⓒ prevented

Ⓓ slowed down

4. Why are the orchards "sagging" and "steamed with amber spice"?

Ⓐ The weather is hot and steamy.

Ⓑ The trees are heavy with ripe fruit.

Ⓒ The fields have gone completely wild.

Ⓓ The farmers have started a fire in the orchard.

5. What told the geese it was time to go?

Ⓐ clues left behind from last year

Ⓑ a mysterious messenger

Ⓒ other wild animals

Ⓓ the signs of nature

Understanding the Poem

If you say this poem aloud to yourself, you should feel an accent on some of the syllables in each line. Circle each accented syllable. Sometimes, you will circle the whole word. The first line has been done for you. Read the poem aloud to yourself or a partner to check your work.

(Something) (told) the (wild) (geese)

it was time to go,

Though the fields lay golden

Something whispered, "Snow!"

Leaves were green and stirring,

Berries lustre-glossed,

But beneath warm feathers

Something cautioned, "Frost!"

All the sagging orchards

Steamed with amber spice,

But each wild beast stiffened

At remembered ice.

Something told the wild geese

It was time to fly—

Summer sun was on their wings,

Winter in their cry.

Read and Understand Poetry • EMC 3324 • ©2005 by Evan-Moor Corp.

Poetic Forms

Contents

snowflakes
slip from the sky
like soft white butterflies

Haiku Collection

Before You Read the Poems

Build Background

Read aloud "Worm," the second poem in the collection. Ask students to close their eyes and form a picture of the image that the poem creates as you read it aloud. When you are finished, ask students to open their eyes and share about the feelings and images the poem created. The late-night setting and attention to minute detail may have created a feeling of peace and quiet. Tell students that this is a haiku by the poet Basho. He lived in Japan from 1644 to 1695, and he was a master of haiku. Traditionally, this poetic form was intended to capture the essence of a moment in nature. Some haiku can also be humorous, and this is especially true of modern haiku. The last poem in the collection, "Hiker," is by a contemporary poet, and it shows how haiku can capture the "humorous moment" in commonplace activities.

While You Read the Poems

Ask individual students to take turns reading each of the poems aloud. Remind students that they don't necessarily have to pause at the end of each line. In some cases, a sentence continues from one line to the next. Haiku is too short to establish a rhythm, and it often sounds like a simple statement when read aloud. Encourage students to read each poem aloud several times, experimenting in their delivery to achieve the reading that is most suited to it.

After You Read the Poems

Elements of Poetry

Form: Haiku Write one of the poems on the board and have students help you determine the number of syllables in each line. Draw a slash after each syllable, showing students that the first and last lines have five syllables, and the second line has seven syllables. Ask students to verify that this pattern is followed in all the other poems. They will identify the syllable pattern of "Worm" and "Moon Dance" on the second activity page.

Poet's Toolbox: Detail Detail is the soul of haiku. The haiku poet tries to find that single detail that reveals the most important thing about a particular moment, situation, or experience. With students, apply this principle to each poem in the collection. Ask why they think the poet chose the details he did, and what those details reveal about the particular moment described in the poem. Also ask students why they think this moment was worth writing about. Suggest to students that haiku tries to open our eyes to the beauty, humor, and mystery of everyday occurrences. These poems show us that life is made up of details, and that those details are worth paying attention to.

Follow-up Activities

Students may work independently to complete the activities on pages 50 and 51.

Moon Dance

Men dance round and round.
The moon high above their heads
Is about to fall.

—*Buson Yosa*

Worm

At night, quietly,
A worm under the moonlight
Digs into a nut.

—*Basho*

Clothing

In my new clothing
I seem not to be myself.
Am I someone else?

—*Basho*

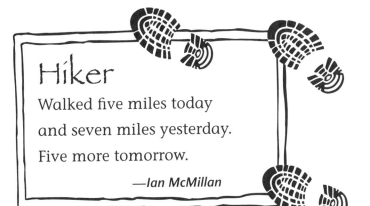

Hiker

Walked five miles today
and seven miles yesterday.
Five more tomorrow.

—*Ian McMillan*

Understanding the Poems

Read each question and choose the best answer. You may wish to reread "Haiku Collection" as you work.

1. Which statement can be said about these poems in general?

Ⓐ They are mostly about thoughts and ideas.

Ⓑ They tell about a simple detail in everyday life.

Ⓒ They are about impossible or imaginary things.

Ⓓ They tell a story with a beginning, middle, and end.

2. Why does the author of "Clothing" feel like he isn't himself?

Ⓐ He is ill.

Ⓑ His clothes don't fit.

Ⓒ He is wearing new clothes.

Ⓓ He is wearing somebody else's clothes.

3. In total, how many miles will the "Hiker" hike?

Ⓐ twelve

Ⓑ fifteen

Ⓒ thirteen

Ⓓ seventeen

4. In each line of "Hiker," the number of miles he must walk _____.

Ⓐ is more than the day before

Ⓑ equals the total number of miles

Ⓒ rhymes with the end of the next line

Ⓓ is the same as the number of syllables

5. In "Moon Dance," why does the poet say that the moon is "about to fall"?

Ⓐ The moon is round and full.

Ⓑ The men are dizzy from dancing.

Ⓒ The dancers are ready to go to sleep.

Ⓓ It is late and the moon is sinking behind the hills.

Read and Understand Poetry • EMC 3324 • ©2005 by Evan-Moor Corp.

Name _____

Understanding the Poems

1. Haiku follows a very precise syllable pattern. Put slashes in "Worm" and "Moon Dance" to show where each syllable is. Then write the number of syllables next to each line.

Worm

At night, quietly,   _____

A worm under the moonlight   _____

Digs into a nut.   _____

Moon Dance

Men dance round and round.   _____

The moon high above their heads   _____

Is about to fall.   _____

2. Now, you try it. Write a haiku poem following the same syllable pattern. When you are finished, exchange your poem with a partner. Count the number of syllables in each line to check your partner's work.

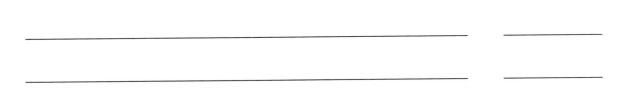

Before You Read the Poems

Build Background

Tanka is a traditional form of poetry that originated in Japan 1,300 years ago. In Japanese, *tan* means "short" and *ka* means "song." Tanka resembles haiku in several important ways. With students, review what they have learned about haiku and ask them to predict what the poems in this collection might be like. They should find that nature and beauty are common themes in tanka, as in haiku. Tanka, however, is known to be a more personal mode of expression than haiku. Whereas haiku zeroes in on a moment in time, tanka is more likely to explore a turning point in a situation, including the feelings and emotions behind it. Ask students to look for other similarities and differences between haiku and tanka as they read the collection.

While You Read the Poems

Tanka poems can be chanted in a songlike manner. Invite volunteers to practice "singing" each poem in the collection. They may actually practice creating a melody for each of these poems, or they may simply let their voices rise and fall in a manner suggested by the poem's meter.

After You Read the Poems

Elements of Poetry

Form: Tanka Longer than haiku, tanka have five lines, as opposed to three, and they are composed of 31 syllables, as opposed to 17. The first and third lines are five syllables each; the second, fourth, and fifth lines are seven syllables each. Like haiku, tanka do not rhyme. Usually, a tanka is divided into two parts, but the division isn't formal. Traditionally, the first three lines form one part, and the last two lines form the second part, but modern tanka don't necessarily follow this formula. The important thing is that the poem opens with a situation, which is followed by a turning point or change of some sort. The "turning point" may also be an insight or revelation about the situation at hand, casting it in a new light. Ask students to identify the first and second part of each poem in the collection.

Poet's Toolbox: Line Breaks Poets don't necessarily break lines at the end of a thought. A line break may come in the middle of a complete thought, or even in the middle of a phrase. Poets use various criteria in deciding where to break a line. In tanka, poets break lines at points that enable them to achieve the 5-7-5-7-7 syllable pattern. With students, examine the line breaks in the poems. Notice how some of the lines break at the end of a phrase, ending with a comma or period, while others break in the middle of a phrase.

Follow-up Activities

Students may work independently to complete the activities on pages 54 and 55.

Midnight Moon

If, by any chance,
I live to be an old man
in this world of woes,
I will never forget how
lovely the moon is tonight.

—Sanjo-no-In

Waves

Waves lick at the shore
sucking at pebbles, shifting
sand, tossing seaweed,
stranding jellyfish. In this
way, waves consume continents.

—Marian Swinger

Pouncer

Still as a statue
The cat awaits her breakfast
An innocent mouse
Carelessly crosses the grass
The cat explodes into life.

—Roger Stevens

Understanding the Poems

Read each question and choose the best answer. You may wish to reread "Tanka Collection" as you work.

1. In "Midnight Moon," what is another way to say "a world of woes"?
  Ⓐ a vast place
  Ⓑ a new country
  Ⓒ a crowd of strangers
  Ⓓ a life full of sadness and worry

2. "Waves" tells how the ocean _____ .
  Ⓐ rises and falls
  Ⓑ tosses and turns
  Ⓒ eats away the land
  Ⓓ is home to many different creatures

3. At the end of "Pouncer," the cat _____ .
  Ⓐ sets a trap
  Ⓑ chases the mouse
  Ⓒ lights a firecracker
  Ⓓ wakes up from a pleasant dream

4. Which of these is <u>not</u> mentioned in "Waves"?
  Ⓐ pebbles
  Ⓑ jellyfish
  Ⓒ seaweed
  Ⓓ coral reefs

5. In "Pouncer," which word lets you know that the mouse has <u>not</u> seen the cat?
  Ⓐ carelessly
  Ⓑ explodes
  Ⓒ awaits
  Ⓓ still

Tanka Collection

Understanding the Poems

1. Tanka poems have a special syllable pattern. What is that pattern?

    a. first line   = _____ syllables   **d.** fourth line = _____ syllables

    b. second line = _____ syllables   **e.** fifth line   = _____ syllables

    c. third line   = _____ syllables

2. Look at the first line of "Pouncer." What's another way of saying "Still as a statue" in five syllables?

_____

3. Look at the second line. What's another way of saying "The cat awaits her breakfast" in seven syllables?

_____

4. Try rewriting one of the poems in your own words. Remember to follow the same syllable pattern. Feel free to make any changes necessary.

_____

_____

_____

_____

5. Now, write your own tanka. First, think of a simple situation. Tell how the situation changes, or how it makes you feel.

_____

_____

_____

_____

_____

Before You Read the Poems

Build Background

The cinquain is a poetic form that originated in America in the early 1900s. It may interest students to know that the cinquain was influenced by haiku and tanka. Like its Japanese predecessors, the cinquain is a short, unrhymed poem. Because it is fairly new, the cinquain has no established or traditional themes. Many poets have experimented with this form, writing on a wide range of topics. The poems in this collection are about nature and the passing seasons.

While You Read the Poems

Read aloud "Gems," demonstrating how to read the poem in a flowing, natural way. Pause at the end of the first sentence, which comes in the middle of the fourth line. Invite volunteers to read aloud the other two poems. Encourage readers to pay attention to punctuation marks in determining where to pause.

After You Read the Poems

Elements of Poetry

Form: Cinquain Explain to students that the word *cinquain* comes from *cinque*, which is the French word for *five*. This may help them remember that there are five lines in a cinquain. Each line has a specific number of syllables:

First line: 2 syllables

Second line: 4 syllables

Third line: 6 syllables

Fourth line: 8 syllables

Fifth line: 2 syllables

Have students verify that the three poems in the collection follow this syllable pattern.

Poet's Toolbox: Similes and Metaphors Introduce students to similes and metaphors, telling them that these are ways of comparing two things. A simile uses the words *like* or *as* to compare. In a metaphor, there is a stronger connection between the two things being compared; they aren't like each other per se, but they are seen as being almost identical. Demonstrate the difference by writing these two sentences on the board: *The snow is like a white blanket;* and *The snow is a white blanket.* The first is a simile; the second is a metaphor. Ask students to find examples of similes and metaphors in the three poems.

Follow-up Activities

Students may work independently to complete the activities on pages 58 and 59.

Read and Understand Poetry • EMC 3324 • ©2005 by Evan-Moor Corp.

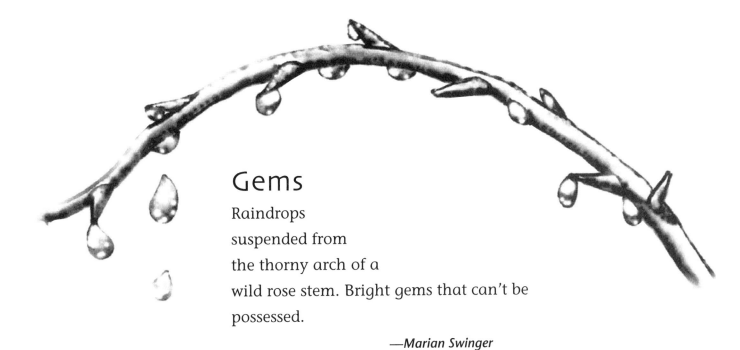

Gems

Raindrops
suspended from
the thorny arch of a
wild rose stem. Bright gems that can't be
possessed.

—Marian Swinger

The Flames of Autumn

Leaves flare,
orange, yellow,
red. Trees blaze briefly and
gloriously before the long
winter.

—Marian Swinger

Spring Snow

Snowflakes
Slip from the sky
Like soft white butterflies,
Brush the trees with their flimsy wings,
Vanish.

—John Foster

Name _____

Cinquain Collection

Understanding the Poems

Read each question and choose the best answer. You may wish to reread "Cinquain Collection" as you work.

1. Look at the first poem. It compares _____.
   Ⓐ rain and fire
   Ⓑ stems and arches
   Ⓒ flowers and thorns
   Ⓓ raindrops and gems

2. In the second poem, the leaves of a tree are described as _____.
   Ⓐ teardrops
   Ⓑ gemstones
   Ⓒ flames of fire
   Ⓓ flakes of snow

3. How are raindrops like gems "that can't be possessed"?
   Ⓐ Gems aren't free, but raindrops are.
   Ⓑ Gems are forever, and so are raindrops.
   Ⓒ Rain is a gift from the sky, and gems are a gift from Earth.
   Ⓓ Raindrops are beautiful, but you can't hold them in your hand.

4. In the second poem, what does *gloriously* probably mean?
   Ⓐ faithfully
   Ⓑ brilliantly
   Ⓒ delicately
   Ⓓ hopefully

5. In the last poem, snowflakes are being compared to butterflies because they _____.
   Ⓐ are impossible to follow
   Ⓑ both slip through the sky
   Ⓒ disappear without a trace
   Ⓓ float as softly and gently as butterflies

58   *Poetic Forms*   Read and Understand Poetry • EMC 3324 • ©2005 by Evan-Moor Corp.

Understanding the Poems

1. These poems use many similes and metaphors. Decide whether each of the following sentences is a simile or a metaphor. Check the appropriate column. Remember:

Simile (uses *like*)

The snow is <u>like</u> a white blanket.

Metaphor

The snow is a white blanket.

	Simile	Metaphor
Raindrops are precious gems.		
The rose's stem is like an arch.		
Trees blaze briefly.		
Their leaves are like flames of fire.		
Snowflakes fly like butterflies.		
Snow brushes the trees with its wings.		

2. What could you compare these things with? Complete the list.

clouds	⟶	pillow
wind	⟶	_____
dry leaves	⟶	_____
bare tree	⟶	_____
stars at night	⟶	_____
line of ants	⟶	_____

3. Write your own similes and metaphors. Use the list you just completed for ideas, or come up with new ideas.

Example: **The sun rested its head on a nearby cloud.**

_____

_____

_____

Before You Read the Poems

Build Background

Tell students that the two poems they are about to read contain hidden messages. Ask students to scan the poems without reading them word for word, looking for the hidden message. They will probably notice that the first letter of each line, when read together vertically, spells a word. Ask students to make predictions about the poems based on their preview.

Build Vocabulary

To prepare students for "Caribbean," explain that Anancy is a trickster character in Caribbean folktales. They may already know Anancy (or Anansi) from African folklore. You might explain that the Anancy stories came to the Caribbean when Africans were enslaved to work in the sugarcane fields of Caribbean islands such as Cuba and Jamaica. Students may already be familiar with reggae music, which is mentioned in the poem, and which originated in Jamaica. You will probably need to tell students that breadfruit (also mentioned in the poem) is a starchy tropical fruit that can be boiled, fried, and prepared in many delicious foods.

While You Read the Poems

Form groups of students and ask each group to read a line of "Caribbean." You might suggest that students state the letter of each line before they begin reading; for example: **C**–*Coral reef and carnival;* **A**–*Anancy, trickster spider man;* and so on. Repeat the same procedure for "Sunbeam."

After You Read the Poems

Elements of Poetry

Form: Acrostic In an acrostic poem, a word or short message is spelled out using the first letter of each line. Review with students that the title of each poem is spelled out in this way. The hidden message in an acrostic is always related to the theme or main idea of the poem. In "Caribbean," all the sights, sounds, and tasty foods described in the poem are from the Caribbean. In "Sunbeam," the words are all associated with the play of light on a river.

Poet's Toolbox: Word Choice Poets try to choose words that are just right. For example, instead of using the simple word *eat,* they may choose from a whole family of more specific words: *nibble, swallow, chomp, devour,* etc. This principle applies whether the poet is searching for the right verb, the perfect noun, or a descriptive word. With students, examine the action verbs, concrete nouns, adjectives, and adverbs in these poems. Discuss how these words make the poems more lively and fun to read.

Follow-up Activities

Students may work independently to complete the activities on pages 62 and 63.

 Read and Understand Poetry • EMC 3324 • ©2005 by Evan-Moor Corp.

CARIBBEAN

C oral reef and carnival,

A nancy, trickster spider man,

R eggae, rap to sunsplash beat,

I ce cone syrup, juicy sweet,

B readfruit fried, tasty dish,

B lue mountain and flying fish.

E merald sea, blazing noon.

A t Christmas poinsettia bloom.

N ight time, come the mango moon.

—Anita Marie Sackett

SUNBEAM

S lip slither

U nder river

N ow a shiver

B ring together

E ach quiver

A s a silver

M irror mirror

—Mary Green

Acrostics

Understanding the Poems

Read each question and choose the best answer. You may wish to reread "Caribbean" and "Sunbeam" as you work.

1. The first poem tells about _____.
- Ⓐ a colorful festival
- Ⓑ life in and around a coral reef
- Ⓒ things to do and see when you're on a trip
- Ⓓ the sights, sounds, and tastes of the Caribbean

2. What does the expression "emerald sea" mean?
- Ⓐ Emeralds come from the sea.
- Ⓑ The ocean is full of treasures.
- Ⓒ The sea is a beautiful green color.
- Ⓓ There's more to the sea than meets the eye.

3. Which of the following things is <u>not</u> from the Caribbean?
- Ⓐ poinsettias
- Ⓑ mangos
- Ⓒ piñatas
- Ⓓ reggae

4. What is the poem "Sunbeam" about?
- Ⓐ the colors of the rainbow
- Ⓑ the play of light on water
- Ⓒ sunrays reflecting off the moon
- Ⓓ a beam of light shooting through space

5. Which of these does the poet compare the sunbeam to?
- Ⓐ a mirror
- Ⓑ candlelight
- Ⓒ a deep river
- Ⓓ a quiver of arrows

Name _____

Acrostics

Understanding the Poems

1. The poems in this collection are *acrostics*. In an acrostic poem, the first letter of each line spells a word when they are all read together.

What are the nine words from the first poem that are used to spell *"Caribbean"*?

_____ _____ _____

_____ _____ _____

_____ _____ _____

What are the seven words that are used to spell *"Sunbeam"*?

_____ _____ _____

_____ _____

_____ _____

2. On each line, write a word that begins with the given letter. Be sure it relates to the main word.

M   moon   A   Alaska

O _____   M _____

O _____   E _____

N _____   R _____

L _____   I _____

I _____   C _____

G _____   A _____

H _____

T _____

3. On a separate sheet of paper, write an acrostic poem using ideas from the previous activity, or start with a new idea. When you are finished, share your work with a classmate.

snowflakes
slip from the sky
like soft white butterflies

Soft, quietly,
worm under the
digs into a nut.
moon

The Trouble with Spaghetti

Before You Read the Poem

Build Background

Tell students that they are going to read a funny poem about spaghetti. Tell them that the shape of the poem is an important part of enjoying the poem. Encourage volunteers to say what they think the poem about spaghetti might look like. Invite students to draw simple shapes on the board representing their ideas. Encourage students to elaborate on how a poem could be written in that shape. Then let students confirm their predictions by looking at "The Trouble with Spaghetti."

While You Read the Poem

This poem definitely invites a humorous reading. The humor can be accentuated by drawing out and shortening certain words, as suggested by the layout of the poem. For example, you might draw out vowels while reading the final line of the poem, making your voice rise and fall like a roller coaster. Invite individual students to play around with their delivery.

After You Read the Poem

Elements of Poetry

Form: Concrete Poetry Tell students that this is a concrete poem. Explain that concrete poems are shaped like the things they are about. Students can surely see that the poem is shaped like a strand of spaghetti. Ask students to speculate about what a poem about a leaf or a hurricane might look like. Students will put their ideas to work on the second activity page.

Poet's Toolbox: Invented Words Point out the words *tizz* and *twizzle* in the poem. Tell students that these are invented words—they won't find them in a dictionary because the poet made them up. Nevertheless, they can guess what the words might mean. Ask students to guess about the meaning of *fearful tizz*. And what about *twizzle?* Might that be the way you twist and spin spaghetti at the end of your fork? Invite students to share any invented words they may have created.

Follow-up Activities

Students may work independently to complete the activities on pages 66 and 67.

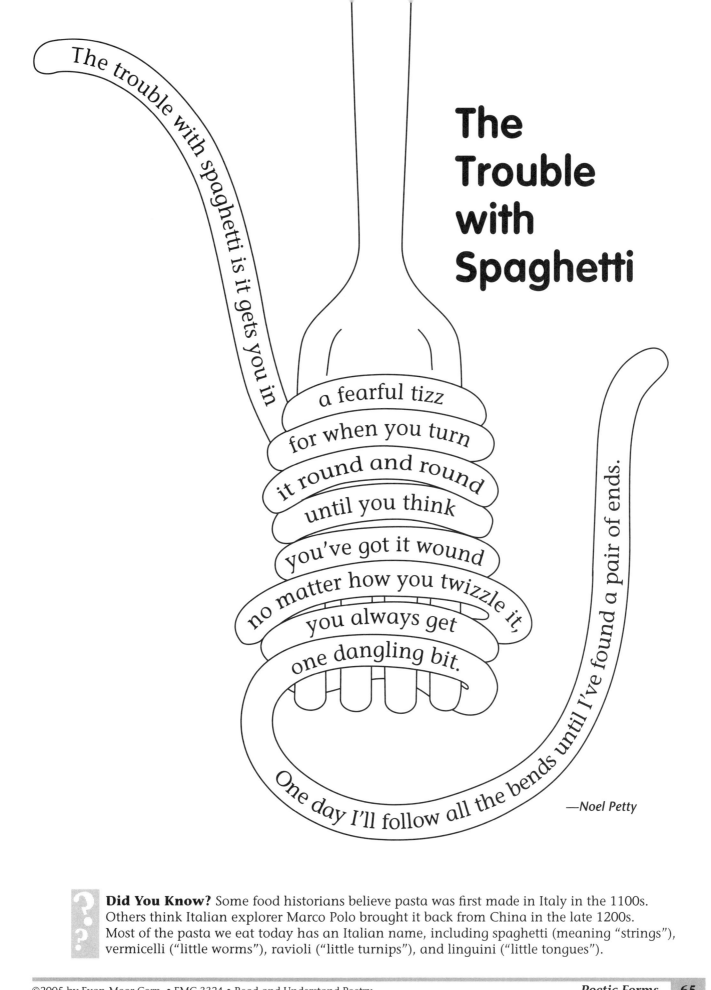

The Trouble with Spaghetti

The trouble with spaghetti is it gets you in
a fearful tizz
for when you turn
it round and round
until you think
you've got it wound
no matter how you twizzle it,
you always get
one dangling bit.

One day I'll follow all the bends until I've found a pair of ends.

—*Noel Petty*

 Did You Know? Some food historians believe pasta was first made in Italy in the 1100s. Others think Italian explorer Marco Polo brought it back from China in the late 1200s. Most of the pasta we eat today has an Italian name, including spaghetti (meaning "strings"), vermicelli ("little worms"), ravioli ("little turnips"), and linguini ("little tongues").

Understanding the Poem

Read each question and choose the best answer. You may wish to reread "The Trouble with Spaghetti" as you work.

1. According to this poem, what is the trouble with spaghetti?

Ⓐ It gets stuck to your fork.

Ⓑ The strands get all tangled up.

Ⓒ Once you start twisting it, you can't stop.

Ⓓ There's always a piece that hangs off the fork.

2. What will the narrator do with spaghetti someday?

Ⓐ Cut the strands in half.

Ⓑ Spin it round and round.

Ⓒ Follow the dangling strands to their ends.

Ⓓ Twizzle the strands until they're untangled.

3. The poem "The Trouble with Spaghetti" is shaped like _____.

Ⓐ spaghetti

Ⓑ a pair of ends

Ⓒ a twizzle stick

Ⓓ dangling bits and pieces

4. When spaghetti gets you in a "fearful tizz," it probably means that you get _____.

Ⓐ scared

Ⓑ frustrated

Ⓒ thirsty

Ⓓ dizzy and faint

5. Which of these would <u>not</u> make a good subject for a concrete poem?

Ⓐ a hill

Ⓑ a slide

Ⓒ a staircase

Ⓓ a bad mood

Understanding the Poem

1. The words *tizz* and *twizzle* are made up. What do you think they mean?

_____

_____

2. Here are some things that don't have names. Make up your own words for them.

    a. a baby ant: _____

    b. the milk and cereal left at the bottom of a bowl:

    _____

    c. an embarrassing mistake: _____

    d. shoelaces that can't be untied: _____

3. "The Trouble with Spaghetti" is shaped like dangling spaghetti. What other shapes might you use for a concrete poem? Remember, the shape helps show what the poem is about.

_____

_____

4. Choose one of the shapes listed above. Write a series of words in that shape. Show it to a classmate and ask him or her to guess what your "concrete poem" is about. If you need more space, use the back of this page.

North, South, East, West

Contents

Before You Read the Poems

Build Background

Tell students that they are about to read two Native American songs. Provide the following background: Before the arrival of European settlers and colonists, there were hundreds of Native American tribes throughout North America. They all had unique cultures and spoke different languages, but there were certain values that they had in common. Honoring ancestors was one of these values. Native Americans revered their ancestors because this practice linked them with their past; it was, in a sense, a gesture of balance. Both of these poems are about ancestors and the world of spirits. One is from the Omaha tribe, which at one time resided in the Central Plains near the Missouri River. The other is from the Chippewa tribe, also known as the Ojibway, traditionally associated with the Northern region near the Great Lakes. Ask students what they may know about these or any other Native American tribes.

While You Read the Poems

Remind students that these two poems are songs, and that they were probably accompanied by a drum or flute. Invite individual students to read the poems aloud in a chantlike rhythm.

After You Read the Poems

Elements of Poetry

Form: Traditional Poetry and Translation Traditional poems and songs are very changeable. As they are passed down from one generation to the next, there may be subtle changes in word choice, arrangements, and emphases. This is especially true when a traditional song is translated from one language to another. There are many valid ways of translating traditional material. Have students suggest other ways of wording certain lines. The first line, for example, could also be stated as follows: *When I listen to the elders*. Students will have more practice with this on the second activity page.

Poet's Toolbox: Voice and Audience Every poem has a perspective. These two poems are told from the perspective of the first person singular, or *I*. This is explicitly stated in the first poem, but how is it achieved in the second poem? Ask students to identify the speaker of the first poem and the "listener," who is not the same as the audience. The speaker and listener in the poem are spirits, but the audience was probably a group of villagers during a ritual or ceremony.

Follow-up Activities

Students may work independently to complete the activities on pages 71 and 72.

Songs of the First Nations

A Song of Greatness

When I hear my elders
Telling of heroes and great deeds
So long ago,
When I hear them talking
About our great ancestors
Then I think to myself
I am one of them.

When I hear others
Praising the great ones,
Then I know that I too
Will be honored
When my time comes, I too
Will do great deeds.

—an Ojibway song

Song of Two Spirits

My friend
This is a wide world
We're traveling over
Walking on the moonlight.

—an Omaha song

Did You Know? At the time of the first contact with white Americans, the Ojibway and Omaha tribes lived in different areas of the Great Plains. Their poems and songs were taught by one generation to the next. The Omaha language is part of a family of Sioux languages. The Ojibway language comes from the family of Algonquin languages. Some of the words that have come into English from the Ojibway language include *Mississippi* (meaning "large water"), *Milwaukee* (originally pronounced *mino-aki*), *moccasin*, and *pecan*.

Understanding the Poems

Read each question and choose the best answer. You may wish to reread "Songs of the First Nations" as you work.

1. The first poem is mainly about _____.
- Ⓐ the way to ask the tribe's ancestors for a favor
- Ⓑ the custom of giving thanks for a good harvest
- Ⓒ how to ask for a good sign before starting a journey
- Ⓓ the tradition of honoring ancestors through the generations

2. What are "elders"?
- Ⓐ ghosts and spirits
- Ⓑ older members of the community
- Ⓒ wonderful tales that are hard to believe
- Ⓓ heroes that have performed great deeds

3. The speaker of the first poem is probably _____.
- Ⓐ a wise old man
- Ⓑ a young person
- Ⓒ the mother of children
- Ⓓ not really a person at all

4. The "friend" in the second poem is probably _____.
- Ⓐ a spirit
- Ⓑ a priest
- Ⓒ a tribal chief
- Ⓓ a stranger on the road

5. These two poems show that Native Americans _____.
- Ⓐ were very competitive
- Ⓑ moved from place to place
- Ⓒ were very good storytellers
- Ⓓ had great respect for the dead

Understanding the Poems

1. These two poems were not written in English. They were written in Omaha and Chippewa, which are Native American languages. There are many different ways these songs can be translated. Practice by matching phrases that mean the same or almost the same.

    _____ great deeds   **a.** a pair of ghosts roaming at night

    _____ I will be honored   **b.** giving thanks

    _____ in ancient times   **c.** heroic actions

    _____ old men   **d.** many, many years ago

    _____ showing gratitude   **e.** people will respect me

    _____ two wandering spirits **f.** tribal elders

2. Now, write your own version of "A Song of Greatness." Change the wording as you like. You may also change the order of the words. Share your "translation" with a partner.

A Song of Greatness

When I hear my elders _____ When I hear the old ones _____

Telling of heroes and great deeds _____

So long ago _____ ,

When I hear them talking _____

About our great ancestors _____

Then I think to myself _____

I am one of them _____ .

Read and Understand Poetry • EMC 3324 • ©2005 by Evan-Moor Corp.

Before You Read the Poem

Build Background

Tell students that the following poem is about the Tarahumara Indians of northern Mexico. They call themselves the Raramuri, but foreigners have called them Tarahumara ever since Spanish explorers first gave them this name in the 1500s. Corn is the most important crop of the Tarahumara, and the fall harvest is a major celebration. The Tarahumara are very well known for their ability to run long distances, and they have been invited to join marathons in the United States. This poem celebrates the Tarahumara's way of life.

While You Read the Poem

Read the poem aloud several times with students, exploring its cadence, or inflection in tone, and rhythm. The sound of "pom, pom" may be chanted in the rhythm of a heartbeat. When the class has practiced reciting the poem several times, form two groups of students. Have one group read the text; the other group chants "pom, pom." Students in the "rhythm group" may also want to pat their legs or devise some other percussive sound to mark the beat as they read.

After You Read the Poem

Elements of Poetry

Form: Typesetting Sometimes the placement of text on the page is very important for a poem to take its intended effect. Ask students what they notice about the way the text of this poem is laid out. If necessary, point out that the text is centered on the page. In this way, the words "pom, pom" appear at the center of each line. This emphasizes how rhythm is a central element of the Tarahumara's way of life. The other lines get progressively shorter, and the beat quickens. The reader is tipped off to this by the visual layout of the text.

Poet's Toolbox: Onomatopoeia Draw students' attention to the "pom, pom" that appears in every other line of the poem. Ask students what they think this sound is supposed to represent. They are likely to say that it represents the sound of a drumbeat. The drumbeat, in turn, represents the sound of a variety of activities: hoeing, patting tortillas, and running. Tell students that "pom, pom" is an example of onomatopoeia. It is a word that sounds like the action it represents. Other examples of onomatopoeia are *knock-knock*, *hiss*, and *crash*. Ask students to brainstorm other words to represent the sound of a drumbeat and practice reciting the poem with their new onomatopoeias.

Follow-up Activities

Students may work independently to complete the activities on pages 75 and 76.

I Hear, I Hear

I hear the rhythm of the Tarahumaras
pom, pom,
I hear them hoeing in the cornfields
pom, pom,
I hear them patting tortillas
pom, pom,
I hear them herding their goats
pom, pom,
I hear their bare feet on the land
pom, pom,
I hear them running, running
pom, pom,
I hear their steady drumbeats
pom, pom,
pom, pom,
pom, pom.

—*Pat Mora*

Understanding the Poem

Read each question and choose the best answer. You may wish to reread "I Hear, I Hear" as you work.

1. What is this poem mainly about?

  Ⓐ drums and the rhythm of life

  Ⓑ farmers and harvest celebrations

  Ⓒ the Tarahumara and their way of life

  Ⓓ all the things you can see and hear on a farm

2. Which activity is <u>not</u> mentioned in the poem?

  Ⓐ making tortillas

  Ⓑ planting wheat

  Ⓒ herding goats

  Ⓓ running

3. Which statement about the Tarahumara is probably true?

  Ⓐ They rely on farming for food.

  Ⓑ They don't believe in eating meat.

  Ⓒ They use pompoms at their celebrations.

  Ⓓ They communicate important messages with their drums.

4. Based on this poem, which art form seems to be important to the Tarahumara?

  Ⓐ storytelling

  Ⓑ painting

  Ⓒ weaving

  Ⓓ music

5. Which of the following are used in the poem?

  Ⓐ metaphor and simile

  Ⓑ repetition and rhythm

  Ⓒ hidden meanings in each line

  Ⓓ alliteration and onomatopoeia

I Hear, I Hear

Understanding the Poem

1. In the poem, there are lots of verbs in the *-ing* form. Write the *-ing* form of these verbs. Use a dictionary for help if you need to.

   a. beat _____   **f.** pat _____

   b. cook _____   **g.** plant _____

   c. farm _____   **h.** play _____

   d. herd _____   **i.** run _____

   e. hoe _____   **j.** sing _____

2. The poet uses the onomatopoeia "pom, pom" to represent a lot of different sounds. How would you represent the sound of the following activities? Be creative and make up your own words!

   a. hoeing cornfields _____ thunk, thunk _____

   b. patting tortillas _____

   c. herding goats _____

   d. running barefoot _____

   e. drumming _____

3. What are some sounds of life in the city? Read the list of things that make noise, and then write an onomatopoeia showing the sound it makes. Follow the example.

   car _____ zoom _____   jackhammer _____

   train _____   doorbell _____

   alarm clock _____   ambulance _____

4. On a separate sheet of paper, write a short poem about life in the city using some of the sound words you wrote above. Use this first line to begin:

   I hear the sounds of the city

Before You Read the Poem

Build Background

Tell students that the poem they are about to read is actually a song, and it's from Australia. The author, "Banjo" Paterson, wrote the words for the song at a house party back in 1895. Another guest at the party composed the music. At the time, there was an economic depression in Australia, and many young men were wandering the countryside in search of work. "Waltzing Matilda" tells about life in the Australian bush during hard times.

Build Vocabulary

"Waltzing Matilda" is full of vernacular Australian English. Explain the following terms to students:

billabong: watering hole; small pool adjacent to a stream

billy: camping kettle

coolibah tree: eucalyptus tree

jumbuck: Australian sheep

matilda: a roll of bedding

squatter: a ranch owner

swagman: a man who seeks work while traveling around the countryside

trooper: mounted police

tucker bag: a bag for carrying food

waltz: wander about

waltzing matilda: "hit the road"

While You Read the Poem

Lead students in a choral rendition of the song. If you aren't familiar with the melody, search the Internet for a version of "Waltzing Matilda" that includes a recording of the song and use it to teach students to sing the song.

After You Read the Poem

Elements of Poetry

Form: Lyrics Lyrics are the words to a song. In a songbook, the lyrics are shown along with musical notation. In a book of poetry, as here, only the words are printed. The chorus is a refrain that is repeated after each stanza; the words of the chorus don't usually print after each stanza, however, because they are identical each time. Ask students to identify the chorus of "Waltzing Matilda" and indicate where it would be repeated if the poem were sung as a song.

Poet's Toolbox: Colloquial Expressions Folk songs and popular lyrics often incorporate slang and other kinds of colloquial expressions. Such phrases contribute to the informal, folksy tone that characterizes folk melodies. Review the colloquial expressions in "Build Vocabulary" and ask students to find these words in the song.

Follow-up Activities

Students may work independently to complete the activities on pages 79 and 80.

Waltzing Matilda

Oh! there once was a swagman camped in a billabong,
Under the shade of a coolibah tree;
And he sang as he looked at his old billy boiling,
"Who'll come a-waltzing Matilda with me?"

Chorus:
Who'll come a-waltzing Matilda, my darling,
Who'll come a-waltzing Matilda with me?
Waltzing Matilda and leading a water bag—
Who'll come a-waltzing Matilda with me?

Down came a jumbuck to drink at the water hole,
Up jumped the swagman and grabbed him with glee;
And he sang as he stowed him away in his tucker bag,
"You'll come a-waltzing Matilda with me!"

Chorus

Down came the squatter a-riding on his thoroughbred;
Down came the troopers one, two, three.
"Whose is that jumbuck you've got in the tucker bag?
You'll come a-waltzing Matilda with me."

Chorus

But the swagman, he up and he jumped into the water hole,
Drowning himself by the coolibah tree;
And his ghost may be heard as it sings in the billabong,
"Who'll come a-waltzing Matilda with me?"

—A. B. "Banjo" Paterson

Name _____

Understanding the Poem

Read each question and choose the best answer. You may wish to reread "Waltzing Matilda" as you work.

1. Where does this poem take place?
- Ⓐ in a cave
- Ⓑ at a crossroads
- Ⓒ by the side of a stream
- Ⓓ at the top of a mountain

2. What did the swagman do with the jumbuck?
- Ⓐ cooked it
- Ⓑ put it in a bag
- Ⓒ took it for a ride
- Ⓓ threw it in the water

3. What happened after the troopers came down to the water?
- Ⓐ They waltzed with each other.
- Ⓑ They squatted on the riverbank.
- Ⓒ The swagman jumped into the billabong.
- Ⓓ A jumbuck came to get a drink of water.

4. The swagman probably drowned himself _____.
- Ⓐ for no good reason
- Ⓑ to teach the troopers a lesson
- Ⓒ as revenge against the squatter
- Ⓓ because he was caught stealing

5. This poem tells _____.
- Ⓐ why the billabong is haunted
- Ⓑ how the coolibah tree got its name
- Ⓒ about a brave hero and his great deeds
- Ⓓ what happens when you try to help a jumbuck

Understanding the Poem

In the space provided, draw a picture showing how the poem ends.
Label the coolibah tree, the squatter, the troopers, and the tucker bag
with the jumbuck in it. How will you show the swagman's ghost?

Before You Read the Poem

Build Background

On a world map, point out the country of China and Hong Kong. Talk with students about the busy harbors of this region, explaining that there is a lot of boat traffic. There are so many boats going to and fro that smaller boats service them by selling food and merchandise. A sampan, for example, is a small skiff propelled by two oars, and it may or may not have a sail. If possible, show students a picture of a sampan, such as the one that may be viewed at this Web site: http://www.worldisround.com/articles/20149/photo4.html. Tell students that the poem they are about to read is about a sampan.

While You Read the Poem

Invite partners to practice reading the poem together. As one student reads, the other can tap out the beat created by the words that are repeated at the end of each line at the beginning and the end of the poem. They can tap out the beat using a drumstick, by clapping their hands, or snapping their fingers. When they are finished with the first reading, have students switch roles.

After You Read the Poem

Elements of Poetry

Form: List Poem Point out that this poem is written as free verse, so it does not use any special pattern of rhyme or meter. This free verse poem builds its rhythm by listing a series of noun-verb combinations that form a singsong refrain. Help students see how these listing verses make up the first four and the last four lines of this twelve-line poem. The middle four lines contain the only complete sentence in the poem: "Up and down the long green river/Willow branches brush the river." Here, too, however, a line formed of another noun-verb combination—"Ohe Ohe lanterns quiver"—separates this complete thought, helping to retain the singsong quality created by the listing technique.

Poet's Toolbox: Onomatopoeia Explain to students that onomatopoeia is the use of a word that imitates a sound. *Buzz* and *sizzle* are two examples. Ask students to find other examples of onomatopoeia in the poem, such as *lap*, *clap*, *flap*, and *tap*.

Follow-up Activities

Students may work independently to complete the activities on pages 83 and 84.

Sampan

Waves lap lap
Fish fins clap clap
Brown sails flap flap
4 Chopsticks tap tap
Up and down the long green river
Ohe Ohe lanterns quiver
Willow branches brush the river
8 Ohe Ohe lanterns quiver
Waves lap lap
Fish fins clap clap
Brown sails flap flap
12 Chopsticks tap tap

—*Tao Lang Pee*
translation by
Channing and Olive Wence

Read and Understand Poetry • EMC 3324 • ©2005 by Evan-Moor Corp.

Understanding the Poem

Read each question and choose the best answer. You may wish to reread "Sampan" as you work.

1. This poem _____.
   Ⓐ is a kind of riddle
   Ⓑ is a good example of haiku
   Ⓒ describes the sights and sounds from a boat
   Ⓓ tells the beginning of a story, but not the end

2. In the poem, "flap flap" is the sound of _____.
   Ⓐ birds flapping their wings
   Ⓑ sails on a sampan
   Ⓒ splashing waves
   Ⓓ willow branches

3. In line 6, what does the word *quiver* probably mean?
   Ⓐ silently glide
   Ⓑ rattle and roll
   Ⓒ go underwater
   Ⓓ tremble and flicker

4. Which of the following is an example of onomatopoeia?
   Ⓐ tap tap
   Ⓑ chopsticks
   Ⓒ up and down
   Ⓓ branches brush

5. Which words help you know that the poem takes place on or near water?
   Ⓐ green, brush, tap
   Ⓑ waves, fish, river
   Ⓒ clap, long, branches
   Ⓓ brown, chopsticks, lanterns

Sampan

Understanding the Poem

1. *Onomatopoeia* is the use of a word that sounds like the thing it represents. *Crash* is a good example. It means "high-speed accident," and it sounds like one, too!

   Write the word the poet uses for the sound of each of these:

   a. chopsticks as they click against each other _____

   b. small waves gently coming up to the riverbank _____

   c. fish as they flap their fins open and shut _____

   d. the sails of a boat flapping in the wind _____

2. Write the onomatopoeia that goes with each description.

achoo	buzz	hiss	pitter-pat	splat	whoosh

   a. The sound you make when you sneeze is _____.

   b. The sound of an egg falling on the floor is _____.

   c. A snake's flickering tongue sounds like _____.

   d. A cat walking across the roof sounds like _____.

   e. A bee flying around the room makes the sound _____.

   f. A hawk swooping through the air makes the sound _____.

3. What are some of your favorite onomatopoeias? Write a list of at least four good ones. Show them to a classmate and ask him or her to guess what they represent.

   _____

   _____

   _____

   _____

Read and Understand Poetry • EMC 3324 • ©2005 by Evan-Moor Corp.

Fanciful Fun

Contents

Before You Read the Poems

Build Background

Ask students if they know any limericks and, if so, invite them to recite one or two for the class. If they don't know any by heart, they will have the chance to recite one later on. Then pose the following question: *Where do you think limericks came from?* Answer: Limericks are named after an Irish city by the name of—you guessed it—Limerick! This poetic form is at least one hundred years old, and it may be much older. Limericks became particularly popular at the turn of the twentieth century when newspapers held limerick contests with big prizes offered to the best and the funniest limerick. Limericks have continued to be a popular source of humor ever since.

While You Read the Poems

Many limericks are based in an oral tradition and are told from memory. To help students appreciate the oral aspect of limericks, tell them that you are going to hold a limerick contest. Tell students to choose one of the limericks and memorize it. They will probably need to practice saying the poem aloud for at least ten minutes. Then invite students to take turns reciting the poems for the class. You may want to conduct votes to award prizes in different categories: best memory, best delivery, etc.

After You Read the Poems

Elements of Poetry

Form: Limerick The rules for writing a limerick are not as strict as other poetic forms. Generally speaking, a limerick follows an *aabba* rhyming pattern. Lines 1, 2, and 5 have eight or nine syllables. Lines 3 and 4 have fewer syllables than the rest of the poem—anywhere from five to seven syllables—although both lines should have the same number of syllables. A good limerick sounds like a joke: it is "set up" in the opening lines, and delivers a punch at the end. You might want to check comprehension by having students paraphrase the joke in each limerick, using their own words.

Poet's Toolbox: Tongue Twisters Tongue twisters appear in many different forms: couplets, quatrains, and of course, limericks. They are characterized by the close proximity of consonant-vowel combinations that are easily confused. Ask students to find these troublesome pairs in the second limerick, where the sound *too* appears "open" and "closed" by another syllable starting with the letter *t*. The temptation is of course to "close" the open syllable whenever it appears by adding a syllable starting with *t*. In the last poem, the two words *flea* and *fly* are so similar, and alternate with each other so closely, that they are more than easy to mispronounce. For extra measure, the final line adds several different vowel sounds after the *fl* cluster.

Follow-up Activities

Students may work independently to complete the activities on pages 88 and 89.

Limerick Collection

1

There was a young farmer from Leeds
Who swallowed six packets of seeds.
It soon came to pass
He was covered with grass,
And he couldn't sit down for the weeds.

—*Traditional*

2

A tutor who taught on the flute
Tried to teach two young tooters to toot.
Said the two to the tutor,
"Is it harder to toot, or
To tutor two tooters to toot?"

—*Traditional*

3

A flea and a fly in a flue
Were caught, so what could they do?
Said the fly, "Let us flee."
"Let us fly," said the flea.
So they flew through a flaw in the flue.

—*Traditional*

Understanding the Poems

Read each question and choose the best answer. You may wish to reread "Limerick Collection" as you work.

1. The first poem tells about a farmer who _____.
  Ⓐ planted flowers in his hair
  Ⓑ had grass all over his body
  Ⓒ had too many weeds in his garden
  Ⓓ ate his plants before they had a chance to grow

2. In the second poem, the "tooters" ask whether it is harder to _____.
  Ⓐ whistle while you work
  Ⓑ teach or to play the flute
  Ⓒ teach a kid or a grown-up
  Ⓓ teach two students at the same time

3. In the last poem, the flea and the fly were trapped in _____.
  Ⓐ a flue
  Ⓑ a flaw
  Ⓒ a flap
  Ⓓ a flytrap

4. Which of these is another way to say what the fly said to the flea?
  Ⓐ Go away.
  Ⓑ Come with me.
  Ⓒ What should we do?
  Ⓓ Let's get out of here as quickly as we can.

5. How did the fly and the flea get out?
  Ⓐ The fly led the way.
  Ⓑ The flea followed the fly.
  Ⓒ They flew through a hole.
  Ⓓ They pretended to get sick.

Understanding the Poems

1. A *limerick* is a clever way of telling a very simple joke or funny situation. Summarize each limerick in your own words. Don't worry about using rhyming words, tongue twisters, or clever words.

    a. The first poem is about _____

    _____

    _____

    b. The second poem is about _____

    _____

    _____

    c. The third poem is about _____

    _____

    _____

2. The last two poems are tongue twisters. They use words that have very similar spellings, but they mean completely different things. Do you know what these words mean? Write the words in the box next to their definitions.

flaw	toot	flee	flue	fly	flea	tutor

    a. to help a student with his or her schoolwork_____

    b. to blow through a hole on a musical instrument_____

    c. an insect with two wings_____

    d. a small wingless insect that lives on animals _____

    e. to run away from danger _____

    f. a weak spot _____

    g. a pipe inside a chimney _____

         Fanciful Fun   **89**

Before You Read the Poem

Build Background

Nonsense has a special place in British poetry. With songs like "I Am the Walrus," it can even be said that rock legend John Lennon was a writer of nonsensical lyrics. Lennon's predecessors were Edward Lear (1812–1888) and Lewis Carroll (1832–1898), who are considered to be the original masters of nonsense. This genre is strongly associated with satire and parody, but it often defies any kind of interpretation. Tell students not to worry if they don't understand "Calico Pie," because it doesn't make any sense!

Build Vocabulary

Some of the words in "Calico Pie" are hardly used anymore. Share the following definitions with students, but remind them not to take the terms too literally. Knowing the meaning of *calico* doesn't help in figuring out what a "calico pie" is.

calico: cotton cloth with bright designs

sole: a flat fish

sprat: very small fish such as herrings

syllabub: a gelatin dessert with sweetened milk or cream

While You Read the Poem

Form four groups of students and assign one stanza to each group. Have groups read the poem aloud, one stanza at a time. You may wish to switch groups several times to give students the opportunity to read each stanza. Model the pronunciation of nonsensical words such as *Willeby-Wat* and *Flippity flup*.

After You Read the Poem

Elements of Poetry

Form: Rhyming Verse Most nonsense poetry is written as rhyming verse. The rhymes are what make it sound like it might mean something. Without rhymes, nonsense poetry would be total gibberish. The rhyming pattern of "Calico Pie" is rather sophisticated. Ask students to help you find the pattern, which is *aabcccbddb*.

Poet's Toolbox: Refrain A refrain is a repetitive group of lines, usually at the end of a stanza. Help students identify the refrain in "Calico Pie," which is "They never came back!/They never came back!/They never came back to me!" Ask students to notice how the refrain changes in the second stanza. The pronoun *They* is changed to *He*. The difference is so subtle that it is hardly noticeable, and this is one of the keys to pleasing poetry: the balance between repetition and variation.

Follow-up Activities

Students may work independently to complete the activities on pages 93 and 94.

Read and Understand Poetry • EMC 3324 • ©2005 by Evan-Moor Corp.

Calico Pie

1　Calico Pie,
　The little Birds fly
　Down to the calico tree,
　Their wings were blue,
　And they sang 'Tilly-loo!'
　Till away they flew,—
　And they never came back to me!
　They never came back!
　They never came back!
　They never came back to me!

2　Calico Jam,
　The little Fish swam,
　Over the syllabub sea,
　He took off his hat,
　To the Sole and the Sprat,
　And the Willeby-Wat,—
　But he never came back to me!
　He never came back!
　He never came back!
　He never came back to me!

3 Calico Ban,
The little Mice ran,
To be ready in time for tea,
Flippity flup,
They drank it all up,
And danced in the cup,—
But they never came back to me!
They never came back!
They never came back!
They never came back to me!

4 Calico Drum,
The Grasshoppers come,
The Butterfly, Beetle, and Bee,
Over the ground,
Around and around,
With a hop and a bound,—
But they never came back to me!
They never came back!
They never came back!
They never came back to me!

—*Edward Lear*

 Did You Know? As a young man, Edward Lear wrote scientific books about birds. His books were illustrated with his own paintings. Later, he wrote nonsense poems using the name Derry Down Derry. Today, most people don't know about his bird books, but lots of people still read his poems.

Understanding the Poem

Read each question and choose the best answer. You may wish to reread "Calico Pie" as you work.

1. Why is the author of this poem so sad?

   Ⓐ Nobody likes him.

   Ⓑ It's a dark and dreary day.

   Ⓒ He has to go on a long trip.

   Ⓓ Everybody has gone away.

2. In stanza 2, "Sole" and "Sprat" are probably two kinds of _____.

   Ⓐ fish

   Ⓑ bugs

   Ⓒ birds

   Ⓓ trees

3. In stanza 3, "Flippety flup" is the sound of _____.

   Ⓐ singing birds

   Ⓑ mice drinking tea

   Ⓒ jumping grasshoppers

   Ⓓ fish swimming through the water

4. The last stanza is about different kinds of _____.

   Ⓐ songs

   Ⓑ dances

   Ⓒ insects

   Ⓓ animals

5. This poem _____.

   Ⓐ is partly true

   Ⓑ is hard to understand

   Ⓒ means exactly what it says

   Ⓓ doesn't make very much sense

Calico Pie

Understanding the Poem

1. "Calico Pie" is a poem with rhyming verse. Find all the words in the poem that rhyme and write them next to the appropriate word.

   a. around: _____

   b. ban: _____

   c. bee: _____

   d. blue: _____

   e. come: _____

   f. cup: _____

   g. fly: _____

   h. hat: _____

   i. jam: _____

2. What do you think the following words might mean? Look at the words in the box for help, but you'll have to be creative. The poet made up the words, so use your imagination.

   > **calico:** cotton cloth with bright designs
   >
   > **sole:** a flat fish
   >
   > **sprat:** very small fish such as herrings
   >
   > **syllabub:** a gelatin dessert with sweetened milk or cream

   calico pie _____

   syllabub sea _____

   Flippety flup _____

   Tilly-loo _____

   Willeby-Wat _____

Read and Understand Poetry • EMC 3324 • ©2005 by Evan-Moor Corp.

Before You Read the Poem

Build Background

Ask students if they have ever heard of an animal called the platypus. This animal, also called the duck-billed platypus, is found in Australia and Tasmania. It is hard to classify because it has traits and characteristics of a mammal as well as a bird. The platypus has webbed feet and thick fur; a short, thick tail; and a flat, toothless, bill-like mouth. These traits allow it to live on land as well as in water. It is one of the very few egg-laying mammals in the world. In short, the platypus is a bit of a conundrum. This poem pokes fun at the difficulty scientists have had in classifying this unusual animal.

Build Vocabulary

Explain the following vocabulary to students before reading the poem:

at bay: under control, put to the side

baffle: confuse

derision: scorn, ridicule, criticism

indecision: inability to make a decision

perplexed: confused

vacillating: hesitating between two choices

vexed: puzzled

Note: The scientific name for the platypus is *ornithorhynchus anatinus*, but the poet has made up a new term: *ornithorhynchus paradoxus*. This is a play on the word *paradox*, which is a statement that seems to contradict itself.

While You Read the Poem

Model reading the poem aloud, with emphasis on the correct pronunciation of the more difficult words and terms. Then invite volunteers to take turns reading the poem aloud. Encourage them to use a mock "scientific" tone of voice.

After You Read the Poem

Elements of Poetry

Form: Rhyming Verse This poem is written in rhyming verse. Ask students to help you determine the rhyming pattern, which is *aabbcccddeeff*.

Poet's Toolbox: Capitalization Poets sometimes capitalize words in the middle of a line to make the word sound more important. Capitalizing a common noun almost raises its status to that of a proper noun. Ask students to help you find the common nouns that the author has capitalized.

Follow-up Activities

Students may work independently to complete the activities on pages 97 and 98.

The Platypus

My child, the Duck-billed Platypus
A sad example sets for us:
From him we learn how Indecision
Of character provokes Derision.
This vacillating Thing, you see,
Could not decide which he would be,
Fish, Flesh, or Fowl, and chose all three.
The scientists were sorely vexed
To classify him; so perplexed
Their brains, that they, with Rage at bay,
Called him a horrid name one day,—
A name that baffles, frights and shocks us,
Ornithorhynchus Paradoxus.

—*Oliver Herford*

The Platypus

Understanding the Poem

Read each question and choose the best answer. You may wish to reread "The Platypus" as you work.

1. This poem is mainly about _____ .
   - Ⓐ how tricky and clever the platypus is
   - Ⓑ how hard it is to classify the platypus
   - Ⓒ the difference between "Fish, Flesh, or Fowl"
   - Ⓓ the importance of finding the right name for something

2. What does the author mean by "Flesh"?
   - Ⓐ a reptile with scales
   - Ⓑ an animal with feathers
   - Ⓒ an animal with fins
   - Ⓓ a mammal

3. Which of these is another word for *vexed*?
   - Ⓐ jinxed
   - Ⓑ unlucky
   - Ⓒ puzzled
   - Ⓓ frightened

4. Why were the scientists so angry?
   - Ⓐ They held their rage at bay.
   - Ⓑ The platypus wouldn't make up its mind.
   - Ⓒ Someone had called them a horrid name.
   - Ⓓ They didn't know how to categorize the platypus.

5. According to this poem, what is so funny about the name given to the platypus?
   - Ⓐ It's hard to pronounce.
   - Ⓑ It's not spelled correctly.
   - Ⓒ It doesn't make any sense.
   - Ⓓ The author made it up so it would rhyme.

Name _____

Understanding the Poem

1. Animals are grouped into different categories. Mammals are warmblooded animals. They have hair and a backbone. Birds have wings, feathers, and a beak. Fish are coldblooded animals. They have scales, gills, and fins. Sort these animals into the proper category.

cat	duck	shark	owl	tiger
horse	tuna	monkey	goose	trout
salmon	eagle	hummingbird	elephant	goldfish

Mammals	Birds	Fish

2. The platypus doesn't fit into any one of these categories because it has hair, a bill like a duck, webbed feet, and a flat tail. Make up another animal by combining the parts of different animals. Draw a picture of it and give it a name.

Before You Read the Poem

Build Background

Tell students that the following poem is by Lewis Carroll, a famous author of children's literature. He is perhaps most famous for writing *Alice's Adventures in Wonderland.* Invite students to share what they know about this book. Share with students that Carroll also wrote poetry. "The Walrus and the Carpenter" is from a book called *Through the Looking-Glass and What Alice Found There.* The poems of Lewis Carroll are known for being nonsensical. They are fun to read because they are about fantastical characters in absurd situations.

While You Read the Poem

Ask four volunteers to take four different parts in an oral reading of the poem: narrator, Moon, Walrus, and Carpenter. Prompt each student to read his or her lines at the appropriate time. Note that the Carpenter and the Walrus will read a line in unison at the end of the fourth stanza. When the group is finished reading, invite another group of students to take a turn.

After You Read the Poem

Elements of Poetry

Form: Rhyming Verse This poem is written in rhyming verse. The rhyming pattern is very simple: there is one rhyming sound in each stanza. The rhyming words appear on every other line because the lines are broken. In other words, even though there appear to be six lines in each stanza, there are really only three. Poets sometimes break lines when they are too long to fit on a page. When a line breaks, the second part of the line is indented. Ask students to identify the rhyming words and the indented lines in each stanza. Point out that the indented lines should be read without a pause, unless there is a comma at the end of the preceding line.

Poet's Toolbox: Dialog Poets often use dialog when they have created fictional characters and they want those characters to come to life. The lines spoken by each character are enclosed by quotation marks. Review the lines of dialog that students took turns reading during the oral part of the warm-up.

Follow-up Activities

Students may work independently to complete the activities on pages 102 and 103.

The Walrus and the Carpenter

1 The sun was shining on the sea,
   Shining with all his might;
He did his very best to make
   The billows smooth and bright—
And this was odd, because it was
   The middle of the night.

2 The moon was shining sulkily,
   Because she thought the sun
Had got no business to be there
   After the day was done—
"It's very rude of him," she said,
   "To come and spoil the fun."

Read and Understand Poetry • EMC 3324 • ©2005 by Evan-Moor Corp.

3 The sea was wet as wet could be,
　　The sands were dry as dry.
　You could not see a cloud, because
　　No cloud was in the sky;
　No birds were flying overhead—
　　There were no birds to fly.

4 The Walrus and the Carpenter
　　Were walking close at hand;
　They wept like anything to see
　　Such quantities of sand:
　"If this were only cleared away,"
　　They said, "it would be grand!"

5 "If seven maids with seven mops
　　Swept it for half a year,
　Do you suppose," the Walrus said,
　　"That they could get it clear?"
　"I doubt it," said the Carpenter,
　　And shed a bitter tear.

　　　　　—Lewis Carroll
　　　　　an excerpt from
　　　　　Through the
　　　　　Looking-Glass
　　　　　and What Alice
　　　　　Found There

Did You Know? Lewis Carroll was a math teacher at a university in England. His real name was Charles Dodgson. In his spare time, he wrote books for children. His most famous books are *Alice's Adventures in Wonderland* and *Through the Looking-Glass and What Alice Found There.* In *Through the Looking-Glass,* two comical characters named Tweedledee and Tweedledum amuse Alice by reciting "The Walrus and the Carpenter" for her.

Understanding the Poem

Read each question and choose the best answer. You may wish to reread "The Walrus and the Carpenter" as you work.

1. Where does this poem take place?

Ⓐ on a beach

Ⓑ in a castle

Ⓒ on a desert

Ⓓ on the moon

2. In stanza 2, what does *sulkily* probably mean?

Ⓐ sadly

Ⓑ angrily

Ⓒ barely

Ⓓ brightly

3. The moon was mad at the sun because it _____ .

Ⓐ was too bossy

Ⓑ forgot to thank her for an invitation

Ⓒ was shining in the middle of the night

Ⓓ didn't give enough light just when she needed it

4. Both the Walrus and the Carpenter were crying because _____ .

Ⓐ no birds were in the sky

Ⓑ they had to sweep for seven years

Ⓒ the sea was dry and the sand was wet

Ⓓ there was so much sand on the beach

5. The author probably wrote this poem to _____ .

Ⓐ make people think

Ⓑ make people laugh

Ⓒ share a personal experience

Ⓓ communicate something important in a secret code

Read and Understand Poetry • EMC 3324 • ©2005 by Evan-Moor Corp.

Understanding the Poem

1. There are many things in this poem that don't make any sense. In your own words, write about three things from this poem that are impossible.

   _____

   _____

   _____

2. The poet also makes statements that are so obvious that they are ridiculous. What are these four statements? Put the statements in your own words.

   _____

   _____

   _____

   _____

   Now, make three more statements that are just as ridiculous.

   _____

   _____

   _____

3. A *rhetorical question* is a question with an obvious answer. What was the rhetorical question that the Walrus asked? Put it in your own words.

   _____

   _____

   Make up your own rhetorical question about an impossible situation.

   _____

   _____

Stories in Verse

Contents

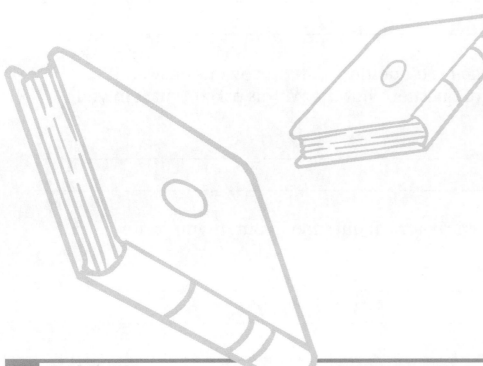

Read and Understand Poetry • EMC 3324 • ©2005 by Evan-Moor Corp.

Before You Read the Poem

Build Background

Tell students that the next poem is about Robin Hood. Ask students what they know about this character. They are probably familiar with him through films, books, and cartoons. Robin Hood was an outlaw who patrolled traveling routes in medieval England. According to legend, he "stole from the rich and gave to the poor." He was often accompanied by a band of "merry men," including Little John, who is also featured in this poem. It isn't known for certain if Robin Hood was a real person, but bandits and highway robbery were definite dangers of traveling in the 1300s. This poem is about a surprise encounter between Robin Hood and one of his relatives.

Build Vocabulary

Explain the following vocabulary and phrases to students. Some of these terms are outdated; others have changed meaning over the years.

bowstring: the string of a bow, used for shooting arrows

gay: brightly colored

sheathed their swords: put away their swords

lea: grassland or meadow

O nay: That's not true.

My pack and all shall gang with thee: You'll have everything I own.

pedlar: an early spelling of *peddler*, a traveling salesperson

perch: a square unit of land

Pray hold your hand: Stop fighting.

thrash: to beat up

While You Read the Poem

Because this poem is lengthy, it is probably best to assign one or two stanzas to different students. Ask a volunteer to read the first stanza, then the next student reads the following stanza, and so on.

After You Read the Poem

Elements of Poetry

Form: Traditional Ballad This poem is a traditional ballad. It was sung aloud as a song from memory until it was written down by a folklorist. Literary ballads such as this one have the same metric pattern, or rhythm, and they tell a story.

Poet's Toolbox: Dialog This poem uses dialog to help tell the story, but the speaker is not always clearly identified in the verse. Sometimes the speaker can only be identified by context. As you read the poem aloud, check to see that students understand who is speaking each line of dialog.

Follow-up Activities

Students may work independently to complete the activities on pages 109 and 110.

The Bold Pedlar and Robin Hood

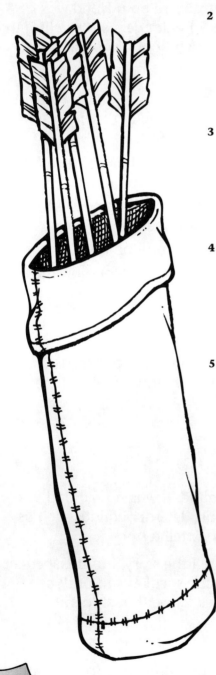

1 There chanced to be a Pedlar bold,
   A Pedlar bold there chanced to be;
   He put his pack all on his back,
   And so merrily trudged over the lea.

2 By chance he met two troublesome men,
   Two troublesome men they chanced to be,
   The one of them was bold Robin Hood,
   And the other was Little John so free.

3 "O Pedlar, Pedlar, what is in thy pack?
   Come speedily and tell to me."
   "I've several suits of the gay green silks,
   And silken bowstrings by two or three."

4 "If you have several suits of gay green silk,
   And silken bowstrings two or three
   Then, by my body," cries Little John,
   "One half of your pack shall belong to me."

5 "O nay, O nay," said the Pedlar bold,
   "O nay, O nay, that can never be
   For there's never a man from fair Nottingham,
   Can take one half my pack from me."

6 Then the Pedlar he pulled off his pack,
And put it a little below his knee,
Saying, "If you do move me one perch from this,
My pack and all shall gang with thee."

7 Then Little John he drew his sword,
The Pedlar by his pack did stand,
They fought until they both did sweat,
Till he cried, "Pedlar, pray hold your hand."

8 Then Robin Hood he was standing by,
And he did laugh most heartily,
Saying, "I could find a man of smaller scale,
Could thrash the Pedlar and also thee."

9 "Go you try, master," says Little John,
"Go you try, master, most speedily,
For by my body," says Little John,
"I am sure this night you will know me."

10 Then Robin Hood he drew his sword,
And the Pedlar by his pack did stand;
They fought till the blood in streams did flow,
Till he cried, "Pedlar, pray hold your hand."

11 "O Pedlar, Pedlar, what is thy name?
Come speedily and tell to me."
"Come, my name I ne'er will tell,
Till both your names you have told to me."

12 "The one of us is bold Robin Hood,
    And the other is Little John so free."
    "Now," says the Pedlar, "it lays to my good will,
    Whether my name I choose to tell to thee."

13 "I am Gamble Gold of the gay green woods,
    And I travelled far beyond the sea,
    For killing a man in my father's land,
    And from my country was forced to flee."

14 "If you are Gamble Gold of the gay green woods,
    And travelled far beyond the sea,
    You are my mother's own sister's son,
    What nearer cousins can we be?"

15 They sheathed their swords, with friendly words,
    So merrily they did agree,
    They went to a tavern and there they dined,
    And cracked bottles most merrily.

—*Traditional*

Understanding the Poem

Read each question and choose the best answer. You may wish to reread "The Bold Pedlar and Robin Hood" as you work.

1. Where does this poem take place?

   Ⓐ on a country road

   Ⓑ on the high seas

   Ⓒ at a circus

   Ⓓ at a hotel

2. The Pedlar was carrying _____.

   Ⓐ a pack of food

   Ⓑ green stockings

   Ⓒ bows and arrows

   Ⓓ suits and strings made out of silk

3. Robin Hood and Little John wanted to _____.

   Ⓐ sell the Pedlar some trinkets

   Ⓑ help the Pedlar find his way

   Ⓒ rob the Pedlar of his belongings

   Ⓓ make the Pedlar join their gang

4. What happened after the Pedlar told his name?

   Ⓐ Robin Hood drew his sword.

   Ⓑ They all went to a tavern.

   Ⓒ Robin Hood told the Pedlar his name, too.

   Ⓓ The Pedlar and Little John got into a fight.

5. Robin Hood and the Pedlar made up because they _____.

   Ⓐ were related

   Ⓑ hated each other

   Ⓒ had the same name

   Ⓓ lived in the same town

Understanding the Poem

1. This poem tells a story. Make a story map telling about each part of the story. Tell each part in your own words.

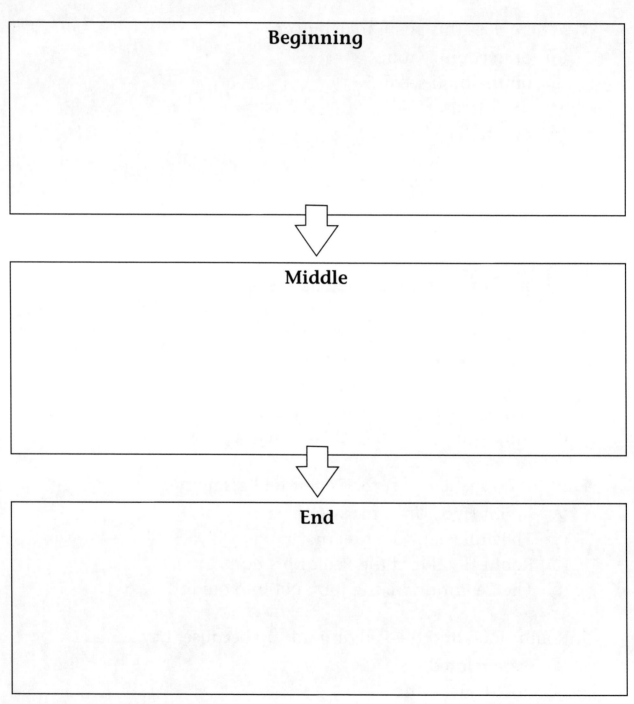

Beginning

Middle

End

2. Now, use the story map to retell the story to a classmate. While you're telling the story, you can include other details that you didn't write about. You can even make up some new details of your own!

Before You Read the Poem

Build Background

Tell students that the following poem is about Hiawatha, a Native American tribal leader, and invite students to share what they know about him. In your discussion, include the following information: In the 1400s, Native American tribes in the Northeast had been engaged in intertribal warfare for decades. Hiawatha helped to stop the fighting by founding the Iroquois League. His stature as a leader is legendary. Longfellow's poem, "Hiawatha's Childhood," has contributed to the mythic character of the stories that surround him.

Build Vocabulary

Explain the following vocabulary to students:

brakes: thickets

dusk: the time of day right before and after sunset

ere: before

fretful wail: a high-pitched crying sound

linden cradle: a cradle made out of wood from the linden tree

lull: to calm a baby to sleep

perish: wither and die

plumes: feathers

reindeer sinews: the tendons of reindeer, which were used as thread

rushes: tall reeds

tresses: braids or locks of hair

wigwam: This word is from the Abenaki tribe. It refers to the round or oval bark-covered dwellings that were typical of Native Americans living in the Northeast. Settlers used this term to describe any Native American dwelling, and it is now considered to be pejorative.

While You Read the Poem

Ask for four volunteers to take the roles of narrator, Hiawatha, Nokomis, and the forces of nature (the pine tree and water). Prompt each student to read his or her lines at the appropriate time.

After You Read the Poem

Elements of Poetry

Form: Narrative Verse This poem, like the others in this unit, is a narrative—it tells a story. As you read the poem aloud with students, pause at the end of each stanza and have students summarize what has happened.

Poet's Toolbox: Contractions In order to achieve the desired number of syllables in a given line, poets sometimes contract a word using an apostrophe, thereby shortening the word by one syllable. As you read, ask students to look for the words *'Tis* and *whene'er*. These are abbreviations for *It is* and *whenever*.

Follow-up Activities

Students may work independently to complete the activities on pages 116 and 117.

Hiawatha's Childhood

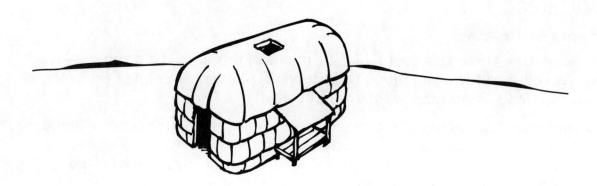

1 By the shores of Gitche Gumee,
By the shining Big-Sea-Water,
Stood the wigwam of Nokomis,
Daugher of the Moon, Nokomis.
Dark behind it rose the forest,
Rose the black and gloomy pine-trees,
Rose the firs with cones upon them;
Bright before it beat the water,
Beat the clear and sunny water,
Beat the shining Big-Sea-Water.

2 There the wrinkled old Nokomis
Nursed the little Hiawatha,
Rocked him in his linden cradle,
Bedded soft in moss and rushes,
Safely bound with reindeer sinews;
Stilled his fretful wail by saying,
"Hush! the Naked Bear will hear thee!"
Lulled him into slumber, singing,
"Ewa-yea! my little owlet!
Who is this, that lights the wigwam?
With his great eyes lights the wigwam?
Ewa-yea! my little owlet!"

Read and Understand Poetry • EMC 3324 • ©2005 by Evan-Moor Corp.

3 Many things Nokomis taught him
  Of the stars that shine in heaven;
  Showed him Ishkoodah, the comet,
  Ishkoodah, with fiery tresses;
  Showed the Death-Dance of the spirits,
  Warriors with their plumes and war-clubs,
  Flaring far away to northward
  In the frosty nights of winter;
  Showed the broad white road in heaven,
  Pathway of the ghosts, the shadows,
  Running straight across the heavens,
  Crowded with the ghosts, the shadows.

4 At the door on summer evenings,
  Sat the little Hiawatha;
  Heard the whispering of the pine-trees,
  Heard the lapping of the waters,
  Sounds of music, words of wonder;
  "Minne-wawa!" said the pine-trees,
  "Mudway-aushka!" said the water.

5 Saw the fire-fly Wah-wah-taysee,
  Flitting through the dusk of evening,
  With the twinkle of its candle
  Lighting up the brakes and bushes,
  And he sang the song of children,
  Sang the song Nokomis taught him:
  "Wah-wah-taysee, little fire-fly,
  Little flitting, white-fire insect,
  Little, dancing, white-fire creature,
  Light me with your little candle,
  Ere upon my bed I lay me,
  Ere in sleep I close my eyelids!"

6 Saw the moon rise from the water,
Rippling, rounding from the water,
Saw the flecks and shadows on it
Whispered, "What is that, Nokomis?"
And the good Nokomis answered:
"Once a warrior, very angry,
Seized his grandmother, and threw her
Up into the sky at midnight;
Right against the moon he threw her;
'Tis her body that you see there."

7 Saw the rainbow in the heaven,
In the eastern sky the rainbow,
Whispered, "What is that, Nokomis?"
And the good Nokomis answered:
"'Tis the heaven of flowers you see there;
All the wild-flowers of the forest,
All the lilies of the prairie,
When on earth they fade and perish,
Blossom in that heaven above us."

Read and Understand Poetry • EMC 3324 • ©2005 by Evan-Moor Corp.

8 When he heard the owls at midnight,
   Hooting, laughing in the forest,
   "What is that?" he cried in terror;
   "What is that," he said, "Nokomis?"
   And the good Nokomis answered:
   "That is but the owl and owlet,
   Talking in their native language,
   Talking, scolding at each other."

9 Then the little Hiawatha
   Learned of every bird its language,
   Learned their names and all their secrets,
   How they built their nests in summer,
   Where they hid themselves in winter,
   Talked with them whene'er he met them,
   Called them "Hiawatha's Chickens."

10 Of all beasts he learned the language,
   Learned their names and all their secrets,
   How the beavers built their lodges,
   Where the squirrels hid their acorns,
   How the reindeer ran so swiftly,
   Why the rabbit was so timid,
   Talked with them whene'er he met them,
   Called them "Hiawatha's Brothers."

—*Henry Wadsworth Longfellow*

Understanding the Poem

Read each question and choose the best answer. You may wish to reread "Hiawatha's Childhood" as you work.

1. This poem tells how Nokomis taught Hiawatha _____.
   A to sing songs
   B to be a leader
   C about the world of nature
   D the names of all the people in their village

2. Nokomis was _____.
   A an owl
   B a fire-fly
   C the spirit of the forest
   D a daughter of the moon

3. What is an *owlet*?
   A a baby owl
   B an owl's nest
   C the eye of an owl
   D the sound an owl makes

4. Which group of animals is mentioned in the poem?
   A fox, turtle, dove
   B fire-fly, owl, beaver
   C hawk, snake, raven
   D eagle, wolf, bear

5. This poem makes you think that Hiawatha _____.
   A disliked nature
   B was a bit of a bully
   C had a hard time controlling his temper
   D was more than an ordinary human being

Read and Understand Poetry • EMC 3324 • ©2005 by Evan-Moor Corp.

Understanding the Poem

This poem tells about the childhood of Hiawatha. Each stanza tells about a different part of the story. Answer each question in your own words. When you are finished, you will have a summary of the poem.

First Stanza: Where was Hiawatha born and what was it like?

_____

Second Stanza: What did Nokomis do to comfort little Hiawatha?

_____

Third Stanza: What kinds of things did Nokomis teach Hiawatha?

_____

Fourth Stanza: When Hiawatha sat by the door of the wigwam for the first time, what did he hear?

_____

Fifth Stanza: What kind of insect did he see, and what did he ask it?

_____

Sixth Stanza: What did Nokomis tell Hiawatha about the moon?

_____

Seventh Stanza: What did Nokomis say about rainbows?

_____

Eighth Stanza: What did she say about the owls hooting at night?

_____

Ninth and Tenth Stanzas: What did Hiawatha do after he heard that?

_____

_____

Before You Read the Poem

Build Background

Tell students that the poem they are going to read is traditionally recited on Christmas Eve. It's about Santa Claus, otherwise known as St. Nicholas. Because students from other cultures may not be familiar with these stories, ask a volunteer to summarize the stories that are generally told to young children about him. In preparation for the poem, make sure that the following is covered: Santa Claus lives at the North Pole, where he makes toys most of the year. On Christmas Eve, he travels around the world in a sleigh pulled by reindeer. At each house, he goes down the chimney with a bag of presents and puts some of those presents under the Christmas tree. After sampling a cookie and a glass of milk thoughtfully laid out for him, jolly St. Nick goes back up the chimney, ready to make his next delivery.

Note: The authorship of this poem has been challenged. For more than 150 years, it has been credited to Clement C. Moore. Recent scholarship indicates that Moore cannot be the author. Instead, it is probably the work of Major Henry Livingston, Jr. He has been credited as the author of "A Visit from St. Nicholas" on the student page.

While You Read the Poem

On Christmas Eve, this poem is often recited by parents to their children, sometimes by heart! Encourage students to memorize parts of the poem. You might ask one student to memorize the first eight lines, another student to memorize the next eight lines, and so on. Invite students to recite their parts in order. Have other students check their written copies to give helpful clues as necessary.

After You Read the Poem

Elements of Poetry

Form: Ballad This poem is a ballad. Ballads are usually written in four-line stanzas called *quatrains*. Often, the first and third lines have four accented syllables; the second and fourth have three. Help students find the accented syllables in the first stanza of this poem. Point out that a stanza doesn't necessarily have to end with a full stop. Some of the stanzas in this poem end in other forms of punctuation.

Poet's Toolbox: Similes Similes are used to compare two things. A simile helps to describe and visualize something. The word *like* is often used in these kinds of comparisons. In this poem, similes are used to describe St. Nicholas after he comes down the chimney. Ask students to look for these similes. They will record them on the second activity page.

Follow-up Activities

Students may work independently to complete the activities on pages 122 and 123.

A Visit from St. Nicholas

1 'Twas the night before Christmas, when all through the house
Not a creature was stirring, not even a mouse;
The stockings were hung by the chimney with care,
In hopes that St. Nicholas soon would be there;

2 The children were nestled all snug in their beds,
While visions of sugar-plums danced in their heads;
And mamma in her 'kerchief, and I in my cap,
Had just settled our brains for a long winter's nap—

3 When out on the lawn there arose such a clatter,
I sprang from my bed to see what was the matter.
Away to the window I flew like a flash,
Tore open the shutters, and threw up the sash.

4 The moon, on the breast of the new-fallen snow,
Gave the lustre of midday to objects below;
When, what to my wondering eyes should appear,
But a miniature sleigh and eight tiny reindeer,

5 With a little old driver, so lively and quick,
I knew in a moment it must be St. Nick.
More rapid than eagles his coursers they came,
And he whistled, and shouted, and called them by name:

6 "Now, Dasher! now, Dancer! now, Prancer and Vixen!
  "On, Comet! on, Cupid! on, Donder and Blitzen!
  To the top of the porch! to the top of the wall!
  Now dash away! dash away! dash away all!"

7 As dry leaves that before the wild hurricane fly,
  When they meet with an obstacle, mount to the sky;
  So up to the house-top the coursers they flew,
  With the sleigh full of toys, and St. Nicholas too.

8 And then, in a twinkling, I heard on the roof
  The prancing and pawing of each little hoof—
  As I drew in my head, and was turning around,
  Down the chimney St. Nicholas came with a bound.

9 He was dressed all in fur, from his head to his foot,
  And his clothes were all tarnished with ashes and soot;
  A bundle of toys he had flung on his back,
  And he looked like a peddler just opening his pack.

10 His eyes—how they twinkled; his dimples, how merry!
  His cheeks were like roses, his nose like a cherry!
  His droll little mouth was drawn up like a bow,
  And the beard of his chin was as white as the snow;

11 The stump of a pipe he held tight in his teeth,
  And the smoke it encircled his head like a wreath;
  He had a broad face and a little round belly
  That shook, when he laughed, like a bowl full of jelly.

Read and Understand Poetry • EMC 3324 • ©2005 by Evan-Moor Corp.

12 He was chubby and plump, a right jolly old elf,
    And I laughed when I saw him, in spite of myself;
    A wink of his eye and a twist of his head,
    Soon gave me to know I had nothing to dread;

13 He spoke not a word, but went straight to his work,
    And filled all the stockings; then turned with a jerk,
    And laying his finger aside of his nose,
    And giving a nod, up the chimney he rose;

14 He sprang to his sleigh, to his team gave a whistle,
    And away they all flew like the down of a thistle.
    But I heard him exclaim, ere he drove out of sight,
    "Happy Christmas to all, and to all a good night!"

    —*Major Henry Livingston, Jr.*

Did You Know? Originally, the names of the last two reindeer were *Dunder* and *Blixem*. The names were later changed to *Donder* and *Blitzen*.

Understanding the Poem

Read each question and choose the best answer. You may wish to reread "A Visit from St. Nicholas" as you work.

1. This poem tells about _____.
   - Ⓐ the mistakes of eight mixed-up reindeer
   - Ⓑ a visit from St. Nick at the wrong time of year
   - Ⓒ a father who catches a glimpse of St. Nicholas
   - Ⓓ two children who spy on Santa Claus on Christmas Eve

2. The action in this poem takes place _____.
   - Ⓐ at the North Pole
   - Ⓑ in broad daylight
   - Ⓒ at St. Nick's house
   - Ⓓ in the middle of the night

3. In this poem, "coursers" are _____.
   - Ⓐ birds
   - Ⓑ reindeer
   - Ⓒ Christmas lights
   - Ⓓ the blades on a sleigh

4. As soon as he came down the chimney, St. Nick _____.
   - Ⓐ called his reindeer
   - Ⓑ bundled up his toys
   - Ⓒ filled the stockings
   - Ⓓ sprang to his sleigh

5. After he left, St. Nicholas probably _____.
   - Ⓐ swept the chimney
   - Ⓑ went to another house
   - Ⓒ wished everyone a happy new year
   - Ⓓ helped the children unwrap their presents

Read and Understand Poetry • EMC 3324 • ©2005 by Evan-Moor Corp.

Understanding the Poem

1. Do you remember the sequence of events in the poem? Write the numbers 1 through 6 to show the correct order of these sentences.

_____ St. Nicholas comes down the chimney.

_____ Everybody goes to bed.

_____ The reindeer land on the roof.

_____ After he goes back up the chimney, St. Nick drives away on his sleigh.

_____ Papa watches St. Nick fill the stockings.

_____ Papa hears a loud noise outside.

2. The poet uses similes to describe St. Nicholas. A *simile* uses the words *like* or *as* to compare two things. Complete each of these similes with a word from the poem.

a. St. Nick's nose was as red as a _____.

b. His cheeks were like _____.

c. His mouth was like a _____.

d. Smoke circled his head like a _____.

e. The beard of his chin was as white as _____.

f. When he laughed, his belly shook like a bowl full of _____.

3. Choose your own words to complete these similes. When you are finished, the sentences will tell a story.

a. The night was as dark as _____.

b. The stars twinkled like _____.

c. Something made a noise that sounded like _____.

d. St. Nick came down the chimney as quiet as a _____.

e. His helpers were as tiny as _____.

f. They climbed the Christmas tree like _____.

Accent

Rhyming verse usually has *meter*, or a pattern of rhythm. The pattern of accented syllables in each line helps set the poem's rhythm. In this example, the syllables where the *accent,* or *stress,* falls appear in the darker boldface type.

Example:

Something **told** the **wild geese**
It was **time** to **go,**
Though the **field**s lay **gold**en
Something **whis**pered, "**Snow**!"

from "Something Told the Wild Geese"
by Rachel Field

Acrostic *(uh-CROSS-tick)*

In an *acrostic* poem, a word or short message is spelled out using the first letter of each line. The hidden message in an acrostic is always related to the theme or main idea of the poem.

Example:

S lip slither
U nder river
N ow a shiver
B ring together
E ach quiver
A s a silver
M irror mirror

"Sunbeam" by Mary Green

Alliteration *(uh-lih-tuh-RAY-shun)*

When several words that begin with the same consonant sound are next to each other or close together, it is called *alliteration*. Note how the poet used the *s* sound in this example.

Example:

Silent, and soft, and slow
Descends the snow.

from "Snow-Flakes"
by Henry Wadsworth Longfellow

Assonance *(ASS-uh-nance)*

When the same vowel sound is repeated in words that are next to each other or close together, it is called *assonance*. In this example, the words *houses, out,* and *about* create assonance.

Example:

Or brought my trees and houses out,
And planted cities all about.

from "The Land of Counterpane"
by Robert Louis Stevenson

Audience *(ODD-ee-unce)*

Sometimes, a poet's words are directed to all readers. In some poems, however, the speaker lets us know that someone specific is being addressed. Those specific readers (or listeners) are known as the *audience* for that poem. In the first example, the audience is a child. In the second, it is a friend of the speaker in the poem.

Examples:

My child, the Duck-billed Platypus
A sad example sets for us
from "The Platypus" by Oliver Herford

My friend
this is a wide world
from "Song of Two Spirits"

Ballad

A *ballad* is a song or poem that tells a story. Most ballads are written in *quatrains*, or four-line stanzas, with patterns of rhyme that help make them easier to recite or sing by heart. Ballads are among the earliest forms of poetry and were used to tell stories and remember events from history. Ballads are still written today, and some are still passed on by word of mouth in the *oral tradition*.

Example:

There chanced to be a Pedlar bold,
A Pedlar bold there chanced to be;
He put his pack all on his back,
And so merrily trudged
       over the lea.

from "The Bold Pedlar and Robin Hood"

Boldface

When words are printed in **boldface**, they are in darker, heavier type. Boldface is used to help words stand out better and add emphasis.

Example:

Black is beautiful
Black is me

from "Black Is Beautiful" by Andreya Renee Allen

Capitalization

The rules for using capital letters and punctuation marks are not always strictly followed in poetry. Some poets choose not to use capital letters at all. In the example shown, the poet did not use a capital *a* in the word *African*.

Example:

I have looked into
my father's eyes and seen an
african sunset.

from "My Father's Eyes" by Sonia Sanchez

Chant

A *chant* is a simple, repetitive rhyme that is meant to be read aloud in a way that emphasizes its strong rhythm. A chant may have a singsong quality to it, or may be based on a traditional song or melody.

Example: Can I, can I catch the wind, in the morning, catch the wind?
Can I, can I catch the wind, in my two hands, catch the wind?

from "Can I, Can I Catch the Wind" by Pat Mora

Cinquain *(san-CANE)*

A *cinquain* is a form of poetry with five lines, each with the number of syllables shown in this example. The word *cinquain* comes from *cinque (sank)*, the French word for *five*.

Example:

Leaves flare,   (2)
orange, yellow,   (4)
red. Trees blaze briefly and (6)
gloriously before the long   (8)
winter. (2)

"The Flames of Autumn" by Marian Swinger

Colloquial Expressions *(kuh-LOW-kwee-ul)*

Informal language and vocabulary that is part of everyday speech is referred to as *colloquial* language. *Colloquial expressions* include slang and familiar expressions. They are often used when a poet wants to reach simple, "regular" people or to represent them in a poem. In this case, the poet used colloquial expressions from Australia to describe how a wandering sheep-shearer steals a sheep to eat. The colloquial expressions are underlined:

Example: Up jumped the <u>swagman</u> and grabbed him with glee;
And he sang as he <u>stowed him away</u> in his <u>tucker bag</u>

from "Waltzing Matilda" by A. B. "Banjo" Paterson

Comparison and Contrast

When two things are compared, the writer points out differences between them. Often, noticing the contrast between two things helps readers "see" what the poet is trying to show them. In this example, the poet compares a moth and a butterfly.

Example: One traveled by day, the other by night
to get where they were going.

from "Caterpillar Race" by John Himmelman

Concrete Poem

A poem that is written with words that form a shape is called a *concrete poem*. Usually, the shape of the poem is similar to the subject of the poem, as in this poem about eating spaghetti.

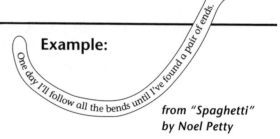

Example:

One day I'll follow all the bends until I've found a pair of ends.

from "Spaghetti" by Noel Petty

Contraction

When poets use a pattern of meter or rhythm, they may shorten a word so it fits the pattern. One way is by taking out a syllable and putting in an apostrophe. This creates a *contraction*, or shortened word, as in the example below where the word *whenever* has been shortened:

Example: Talked with them whene'er he met them,
Called them "Hiawatha's Chickens."

from "Hiawatha's Childhood" by Henry Wadsworth Longfellow

Dialog

When two or more characters have a conversation, it is called a *dialog*. Dialog can be included in poetry; when it is, some poets follow the same rules of punctuation used for writing dialog in prose (quotation marks, commas, and speaker words). Some poets do not.

Example:

"Do you suppose," the Walrus said,
"That they could get it clear?"
"I doubt it," said the Carpenter,
And shed a bitter tear.

from "The Walrus and the Carpenter" by Lewis Carroll

Free Verse

When a poem is written without a pattern of rhyme, meter, or line length, it is called *free verse*. Poets use words and images to help make free verse feel different from regular sentences, or *prose*.

Example:

blue is nice,
and orange is neat
but they can't compete

from "Black Is Beautiful"
by Andreya Renee Allen

Haiku *(hi-KOO)*

Haiku is a form of poetry that first began in Japan in the 1700s. A haiku always has three lines. In the "classic" form, the first and third lines have five syllables, and the second line has seven. A traditional haiku focuses on an image in nature. Even when haiku does not focus on nature, it usually presents a close-up look at a single detail.

Example:

At night, quietly,   (5)
A worm under the moonlight   (7)
Digs into a nut.   (5)

"Worm"
by Basho

Homophones *(HOME-uh-fones)*

Homophones are pairs of words that sound the same even though they're spelled differently, such as *sun* and *son* or *through* and *threw*. Poets sometimes use homophones to create rhyming pairs.

Example:

Winter, I wish I knew
The way you make
Each snowflake new,

from "I Wish I Knew"
by Beverly McLoughland

Limerick *(LIH-muh-rick)*

Limericks are silly rhymes that follow the specific rhyme scheme shown in this example. Limericks always follow the pattern of meter shown here with boldface.

Example:

A **tu**tor who **taught** on the **flute**	*a*
Tried to **teach** two young **toot**ers to **toot**.	*a*
Said the **two** to the **tu**tor,	*b*
"Is it **hard**er to **toot**, or	*b*
To **tu**tor two **toot**ers to **toot**?"	*a*

Traditional limerick

Lyric Poetry *(LIH-rick)*

Poetry that focuses on feelings and impressions is called *lyric poetry*. When they read a lyric poem, readers may think about similar feelings and experiences they have had, or they may imagine the feelings described by the poet.

Example:

Winter,
I wish I knew
The secret of your mind.

from "I Wish I Knew"
by Beverly McLoughland

Lyrics (LIH-rix)

When the words of a poem are set to music and sung, they are called *lyrics*. Sometimes, the words and the music are created separately and combined later. Sometimes, the words and music are created at the same time.

Example: Who'll come a-waltzing Matilda, my darling,
Who'll come a-waltzing Matilda with me?
Waltzing Matilda and leading a water bag—
Who'll come a-waltzing Matilda with me?

from "Waltzing Matilda" by A. B. "Banjo" Paterson

Metaphor (MET-uh-for)

A *metaphor* compares two things by presenting them as being almost identical. For example, a metaphor that compares snow to a white blanket would say: *The snow is a white blanket.* In this example, raindrops are compared to gems.

Example:

Raindrops
suspended from
the thorny arch of a
wild rose stem. Bright gems that can't be possessed.

"Gems" by Marian Swinger

Narrative Verse

Narrative verse tells a story, or *narrates.* The difference between a narrative poem and a prose story is that the narrative poem is told in verse, so it rhymes.

Example:

Two little caterpillars had a race
down the middle of a long dirt trail.
One was as fast as molasses.
The other was as quick as a snail.

from "Caterpillar Race" by John Himmelman

Nonsense Poems

Nonsense poems are silly rhymes that don't always make sense. Their purpose is to entertain the reader with the sound of the words and the images used by the poet.

Example:

Calico Jam,
The little Fish swam,
Over the syllabub sea,

from "Calico Pie" by Edward Lear

Onomatopoeia (aw-nuh-mah-tuh-PEE-uh)

When a word sounds like the noise or sound that it stands for, it is called *onomatopoeia*. In this example, the onomatopoeia *pom, pom* is used to stand for the sound of the Tarahumara Indians' drums.

Example:

I hear the rhythm of the Tarahumaras
  pom, pom,

from "I Hear, I Hear" by Pat Mora

Personification (per-sawn-uh-fuh-KAY-shun)

When a writer describes something that is not human as having qualities or capabilities that are human, it is called *personification*. In this example, the poet describes trees as if they have bodies that can move like humans.

Example:

But when the trees bow down their heads
The wind is passing by.

from "Who Has Seen the Wind?" by Christina Rossetti

Read and Understand Poetry • EMC 3324 • ©2005 by Evan-Moor Corp.

Quatrain (KWAH-trane)

A stanza made up of four rhyming lines is called a *quatrain*.

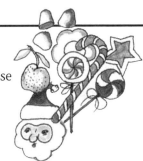

Example: 'Twas the night before Christmas, when all through the house
Not a creature was stirring, not even a mouse;
The stockings were hung by the chimney with care,
In hopes that St. Nicholas soon would be there;

from "A Visit from St. Nicholas" by Major Henry Livingston, Jr.

Refrain (ree-FRANE)

A *refrain* is a group of lines that are repeated two or more times in a poem. When song lyrics include a refrain, it is called a *chorus*.

Example:

And they sang 'Tilly-loo!'
Till away they flew,—
And they never came back to me!
They never came back!
They never came back!
They never came back to me!

from "Calico Pie" by Edward Lear

Repetition (reh-peh-TIH-shun)

When a poet uses the same word or words more than once in a line or in a poem, it is called *repetition*. Repetition can be used to emphasize a word or an idea in a poem. Repetition can also be used to create special sounds or rhythms in a poem.

Example: Can I, can I catch the wind, in the morning, catch the wind?
from "Can I, Can I Catch the Wind" by Pat Mora

Rhetorical Question (reh-TOR-ih-cul KWES-chin)

When a question is not really asked for the purpose of getting an answer, it is called a *rhetorical question.* Sometimes, a rhetorical question is used to say something rather than ask something. When someone says, "Why are you so silly?" it's really another way to say, "You're sure silly!" In the example above from "Can I, Can I Catch the Wind" (see "Repetition"), the poet is using a rhetorical question to help point out that wind is invisible.

Rhyme (RIME)

When two words end with the same sound, we say they *rhyme.* Poets use rhyming words to help make their writing sound different from prose. Rhyme can help words sound special or more musical. Rhyming words are usually placed at the end of a line in a poem. In this example, the first and third lines rhyme and the second and fourth lines rhyme, so we can show this rhyme scheme as *abab.*

Example: Out of the bosom of the Air,   *a*
Out of the cloud-folds of her garments shaken,   *b*
Over the woodlands brown and bare,   *a*
Over the harvest-fields forsaken,   *b*

from "Snow-Flakes" by Henry Wadsworth Longfellow

Simile *(SIH-muh-lee)*

A *simile* compares one thing to another by using the word *like* or *as*. There are four similes in this example.

Example: His cheeks were like roses, his nose like a cherry!
His droll little mouth was drawn up like a bow,
And the beard of his chin was as white as the snow;

from "A Visit from St. Nicholas" by Major Henry Livingston, Jr.

Stanza *(STAN-zuh)*

A *stanza* is a group of lines in a poem. Usually, the lines in a stanza are related to each other in the same way that the sentences of a paragraph "go together."

Example:

Two little caterpillars had a race
down the middle of a long dirt trail.
One was as fast as molasses.
The other was as quick as a snail.
{1}

They started out in early morning—
moved a quarter inch by noon.
By the time they'd gotten twenty feet
they'd turned into cocoons.
{2}

from "Caterpillar Race"
by John Himmelman

Stress *See "Accent"*

Tanka *(TAWN-kuh)*

Tanka is a traditional form of Japanese poetry that developed about 1,300 years ago. In Japanese, *tan* means "short" and *ka* means "song." Like haiku, tanka may focus on nature and beauty. Unlike haiku, it also may focus on feelings. A tanka has five lines: the first and third lines each have five syllables; the second, fourth, and fifth lines each have seven syllables.

Example:

If, by any chance,   (5)
I live to be an old man   (7)
in this world of woes,   (5)
I will never forget how   (7)
lovely the moon is tonight. (7)

"Midnight Moon"
by Sanjo-no-In

Traditional Poetry

The authors of *traditional poetry* are unknown. Traditional poems have been recited and passed down from one generation to the next. Often, these poems were recited for years before anyone wrote them down. There are often several different versions of traditional poems. This traditional ballad is hundreds of years old.

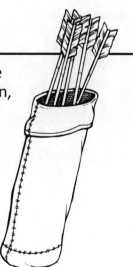

Example: "The one of us is bold Robin Hood,
And the other is Little John so free."
"Now," says the Pedlar, "it lays to my good will,
Whether my name I choose to tell to thee."

from "The Bold Pedlar and Robin Hood"

Folami Abiade

Folami Abiade is an African American poet who has published several books of poetry. Her poetry also appears in a number of anthologies. Originally from Ohio, she is currently an instructor of English and Speech Communications at Bauder College in Atlanta, Georgia.

Andreya Renee Allen

Andreya Renee Allen was born in 1984. Originally from South Carolina, she has traveled extensively and enjoys meeting new and exciting people, especially readers of all types of literature. She wrote the poem in this book when she was a teenager. She has also written for online magazines. Andreya's goals include being a singer, a part-time writer, and the first black president of the United States.

Basho

Basho is the pen name of Matsuo Munefusa, a Japanese poet who is considered the finest writer of haiku. He lived during the mid-17th century, when the haiku form first developed. Basho expressed universal themes using the simple images of nature. His skillful focus on the natural world helped transform haiku from an unimportant pastime into a major form of Japanese poetry.

Lewis Carroll

Lewis Carroll was the pen name of Charles Lutwidge Dodgson, who lived in England from 1832 to 1898, during the reign of Queen Victoria. He was an amateur magician and taught math by profession. Today, however, he is most famous as the author of *Alice's Adventures in Wonderland.* His poetry and stories are characterized by logic and puzzles. His themes are typically whimsical.

Rachel Field

Rachel Field wrote numerous books for adults and children, and was the first woman to win the Newbery Medal. The Association for Library Service presented Field this award for making the most distinguished contribution to American literature for children in 1929 with her long story, "Hitty, Her First Hundred Years," about a wooden early-American doll that Field found in an antique shop.

John Foster

John Foster is a British author. He taught English for over 20 years, and now writes textbooks and poetry anthologies. He has published 8 books of his own poetry.

Mary Green

Mary Green lives and works in London as a writer and children's poet. She has also taught in primary and secondary schools. She likes animals, music, dancing, and riding on the top deck of the bus, at the front.

Oliver Herford

Oliver Herford was born in England in 1863. He spent most of the years until his death in 1935 in the United States. He published over 50 volumes of "light," or humorous, verse and prose. He was also a cartoonist and illustrator. He was known in both his art and his writing for his witty humor.

John Himmelman

John Himmelman is an award-winning artist and author whose work is influenced by his love of nature. He has written and/or illustrated over 50 books for children. He has said, "I've been playing with insects since I was a kid. My interest in moths probably evolved along with my tendency to stay up late at night. The fact that I could find hundreds of different kinds in my own backyard, and that I find their form, function, and beauty a marvel, helped make them an obsession." Himmelman lives in Killingworth, Connecticut.

Edward Lear

Edward Lear (1812–1888) lived in England during the reign of Queen Victoria. He was best known during his lifetime as an illustrator, focusing especially on scientific depiction of birds and other wildlife. Since his death, however, he has become known mainly for mastering the whimsical form known as the *limerick*, as well as for his other humorous poems. While the subject and form of his works vary, nearly all are characterized by an irreverent view of the world. Lear poked fun at everything, including himself.

Henry Livingston, Jr.

Henry Livingston, Jr. was a member of one of the important colonial and revolutionary families of New York. Other descendents from this family include Presidents George Herbert Walker Bush and George W. Bush. During his lifetime, Livingston published most of his poems and prose anonymously or under the pen name "R." Until the year 2000, his most famous poem, "A Visit from St. Nicholas," was thought to have been the work of Clement Clarke Moore. Research, however, showed that the work was actually created by Henry Livingston, Jr.

Henry Wadsworth Longfellow

Henry Wadsworth Longfellow lived from 1807 to 1882. He was one of America's best-loved poets. His poetry is easily understood, with simple, familiar themes. Most people enjoy the patterns of rhythm and rhyme in his poems. He was one of the first artists to use American history, culture, landscape, and traditions as a focus in his art.

Beverly McLoughland

Beverly McLoughland loves to read and write poetry. A collection of her poems has been published, and many of her poems have appeared in magazines and anthologies for children. She often stays up long past midnight writing poetry. It would not be unusual, she says, to find her at the kitchen table, pencil in one hand writing verses, and the other hand reaching for a chocolate donut or a cold glass of milk.

Read and Understand Poetry • EMC 3324 • ©2005 by Evan-Moor Corp.

Ian McMillan

Ian McMillan is an English author who has written a number of poetry books for both children and adults. He has been a poet, broadcaster, commentator, and producer for over 20 years. His poems have been published in numerous magazines, newspapers, and anthologies.

Pat Mora

Pat Mora is an award-winning author of poetry, nonfiction, and children's books. She has published over 20 books for young readers, and often speaks at schools and conferences about writing and multicultural education. A native of El Paso, Texas, she now divides her time between Santa Fe, New Mexico, and Cincinnati, Ohio.

A. B. "Banjo" Paterson

A. B. "Banjo" Paterson was a famous Australian poet whose poems present a romantic view of rural Australia. His ballads and poems are mostly about Australian life, focusing particularly on rural and outback areas. One of his most famous poems is "Waltzing Matilda," but he is also known for "The Man from Snowy River," the inspiration for a movie and a television series.

Tao Lang Pee

Little is known about the life of Chinese poet Tao Lang Pee, who was born in 403 B.C. The poem in this book, "Sampan," appears to have been introduced to the Western world by the noted British playwright, Noel Coward. Coward included translations of three poems by Tao Lang Pee in an anthology of poems first published in 1932. The rich and varied Asian images of Tao Lang Pee's poetry can be found today in several poetry collections.

Noel Petty

Noel Petty is a contemporary British poet. His work has been published in online and print collections. Much of his work is characterized by his uniquely British dry wit. Mr. Petty writes for young people as well as adults.

Christina Rossetti

Christina Rossetti was one of the more important English women poets of the Victorian era. She came from an artistic and religious family; all of her brothers were writers or painters. A somber, religious tone can be found in much of her poetry. She often wrote about unhappy love and death.

Anita Marie Sackett

Anita Marie Sackett has taught for over 25 years in primary and secondary schools in England, New Zealand, and Jamaica. She enjoys all sports and has played hockey for the Jamaican national team. She enjoys sharing her enthusiasm for poetry and gives poetry performances to both adults and children.

Sonia Sanchez

Sonia Sanchez is a retired professor in the departments of English and Women's Studies at Temple University in Philadelphia, Pennsylvania. She has written several plays and is a powerful advocate for black studies programs. Her themes often are feminist in orientation and celebrate women in general.

Sanjo-no-In

The tanka "Midnight Moon" by Sanjo-no-In is often included in collections of the best examples of Japanese tanka poetry. This poem has also been published in English in similar collections.

Roger Stevens

Roger Stevens is a contemporary English poet. He was trained as a fine artist and now teaches part time in Nottingham. He holds workshops on creative writing, poetry, and music, and plays in a rock band. According to Stevens, his free-time activities include "growing feathers" and collecting moss and door numbers.

Robert Louis Stevenson

Robert Louis Stevenson is best known today as the author of adventure novels, especially *Treasure Island, Kidnapped,* and *The Strange Case of Dr. Jekyll and Mr. Hyde.* During his childhood, Stevenson was ill with tuberculosis, and he spent many long days in bed composing stories and reading. In an attempt to improve his health, he traveled to warmer countries. Those experiences provided rich material for his writing.

Marian Swinger

Marian Swinger is a full-time photographer who lives outside London, England. In addition to writing poetry, she enjoys reading, painting, and walking in the countryside.

Buson Yosa

Buson Yosa was a leading haiku poet of the late 18th century and is one of the most well-known poets of this form. Although Buson tried to write in the style of Basho, his own poetry is clearly different and quite varied. He was also a painter, and the influence of his painting can be seen in the imagery of his poems.

Read and Understand Poetry • EMC 3324 • ©2005 by Evan-Moor Corp.

My Read & Understand

Poetry
Anthology

This book belongs to:

_____

Online Resources

The Academy of American Poets: http://www.poets.org

This comprehensive Web site includes over 1,400 poems, 500 poet biographies, and 100 audio clips of 20th- and 21st-century poets reading their own works (e.g., Gwendolyn Brooks, E. E. Cummings, Robert Frost, Langston Hughes, William Carlos Williams, and others). This site also includes the following:

- the Online Poetry Classroom, with free access to poetry curriculum units and other educational resources for teachers

- the National Poetry Almanac and Calendar, which track poetry-related events nationwide throughout the year

- information on National Poetry Month (April)

Lee & Low Books: http://www.leeandlow.com

Publishers of multicultural literature for children, Lee & Low Books has excellent poetry-related material on the Poetry Power page of their Web site. You'll find the following:

- ideas for bringing poetry into the classroom, by poet Pat Mora and literacy educator Regie Routman

- information on additional resources for incorporating poetry into primary classrooms

- digital movies of contemporary poets of color reading their works, including Tony Medina reading "My Grandmother Had One Good Coat" (included in *Read and Understand Poetry, Grades 5–6*) and Pat Mora reading "Song to Mothers" (included in *Read and Understand Poetry, Grades 2–3)*.

Audio Resources

In Their Own Voices—A Century of Recorded Poetry, ©1996, WEA/Atlantic/Rhino

This four-CD boxed set includes 122 poems recorded by their authors, including Robert Frost, Walt Whitman, William Carlos Williams (reading "The Red Wheelbarrow," included in *Read and Understand Poetry, Grades 5–6*), and contemporary poets such as Maya Angelou, Lucille Clifton, Gary Snyder, Carmen Tafolla, and others. In compiling this impressive collection, poetry historian and recording producer Rebekah Presson drew from the Library of Congress archives, poets' personal archives, and recordings made on her 1980s radio show, *New Letters on the Air*. The collection also includes a printed booklet with additional information. Check your public library for a copy of this excellent collection.

The Writer's Almanac®

This is a short program (about five minutes in length) of poetry and history hosted by Garrison Keillor, heard daily on public radio stations. Check their Web site at http:writersalmanac. publicradio.org for local station listings. The Web site also has searchable archives.

Print Resources

Writing Poetry with Children by Jo Ellen Moore, ©1999 by Evan-Moor Corporation

Step-by-step lessons provide guidance for introducing a variety of poetic forms and supporting primary-age students in producing original poetry in each form.

Teaching 10 Fabulous Forms of Poetry by Paul Janeczko, ©2000 by Scholastic

Geared for intermediate grades (4–8), this volume introduces 10 poetic forms and supports students in planning and writing original poetry in each form.

See also the many fine poetry resource books listed on the Web sites noted above.

in daddy's arms
Page 8
1. A—big brother
2. B—spins around in daddy's arms
3. B—at the same level
4. B—how the narrator feels when with his or her father
5. D—spends a lot of time together

Page 9
Answers will vary in wording, but should relate the following meanings:
1. safe and loved.
2. lifts her up and lets her see farther than she can see on her own.
3. she thinks that even the moon is smiling at her.
4. she is shorter than everybody else unless her father picks her up.
5. he spends time with his children and likes to play with them.

Black Is Beautiful
Page 12
1. D—skin color
2. A—is black
3. C—They aren't as beautiful as black.
4. A—proud
5. B—Be proud of who you are.

Page 13
1. black, beautiful, tall, dark, wonderful
2. Answers will vary.
3. Answers will vary.
4. Answers will vary.

My Father's Eyes
Page 16
1. C—the poet's African heritage
2. B—African American
3. D—not mentioned in the poem
4. D—the family's African homeland
5. A—The poet has never met her father.

Page 17
1. Her ancestors are from Africa. When she looks at her father, she can see her African roots.
2. Answers will vary.
3. Answers will vary.
4. Answers will vary.
5. Answers will vary. Example: The language we teach our children is an important link from one generation to the next. Through language, we pass on stories and sayings that contain important values and lessons. We can also save photos, letters, and home movies to share with our children, nieces, and nephews. These kinds of things can help explain "what it was like" in the past.

The Land of Counterpane
Page 20
1. A—on a bed
2. B—sick
3. D—an adult looking back on his childhood
4. A—stayed in bed
5. C—a make-believe world

Page 21
1. He pretends that his pillows are hills.
   His sheets look like waves in the ocean.
   His bedspread, or counterpane, turns into "a dale and plain."
2. Answers will vary. An example might be:
   rug=magical kingdom
   mirror=ice
   fireplace=cave
   sink=whirlpool
   salt and pepper shakers=king and queen
3. Answers will vary. Examples might include:
   fleet/feet
   head/bed
   out/shout
   day/play
   go/show

I Wish I Knew
Page 25
1. D—one of the four seasons
2. C—why each snowflake is so unique
3. A—is a human being
4. A—winter
5. D—impossible to understand completely

Page 26
Answers will vary. Examples:
Winter: freezes ponds and lakes
covers the sun
chases away the birds
plucks leaves from the trees
Spring: thaws the ice
plants flowers
blows the clouds away
lays a green carpet on the hills
Summer: turns up the heat
calls you outside
dries up all the ponds and streams
fills our baskets with fruits and vegetables
Fall: makes leaves turn and fall
tells the birds it's time to go
gives us nuts and squash
whispers and rustles

Can I, Can I, Catch the Wind
Page 29
1. C—as a list of questions
2. B—asks questions that have obvious answers
3. C—a fishing net
4. D—entertain
5. A—The wind can't be seen or held.

Page 30
1. A rhetorical question is a question that is asked for effect; no answer is expected.
2. The answers to the questions are all "no." No matter what you use, you can't catch the wind because the wind has no shape. It's just moving air.
3. The poet asks rhetorical questions to get the reader to see that the wind is mysterious and playful.

4. Answers will vary. An example might be:
   a. sunbeam: Can I ride a sunbeam?
   b. star: Can I touch a star?
   c. lightning bolt: Can I hold a lightning bolt?
   d. night: Can I keep the night?
   e. water: Can I build a castle with water?
   f. sand: Can I count the sand?
5. Poems will vary.

Who Has Seen the Wind?
Page 33
1. B—powerful and mysterious
2. C—through
3. D—not you and not I
4. B—You can't see the wind, but you can feel its presence.
5. C—has a deep appreciation for nature

Page 34
Answers will vary.

Caterpillar Race
Page 37
1. D—a race between a butterfly and a moth
2. C—cocoons
3. C—very slow
4. A—almost two years
5. D—It is partly based on facts but is mostly made up.

Page 38
1. as fast as molasses; as quick as a snail
2. Answers will vary. Examples: wind and clouds, sun and moon, day and night, two different animals, etc.
3. Answers will vary.
4. Responses will vary.

Snow-flakes
Page 41
1. C—a field in the winter
2. D—over the woods and then over a field
3. B—high in the sky
4. D—a dress with folds
5. C—abandoned

Page 42

1. *brown* and *bare* circled

2. The letter *s* should be circled in each word that it appears.

3. Answers will vary. An example could be:

   Green grass grows in the grove.

   The *tall* trees twist and turn in the tornado.

   A *beautiful/blue* butterfly brushed by me.

   She sells *seashells* by the seashore.

4. Answers will vary. Examples could be:

   clouds: Cold and calm clouds come from afar.

   woodlands: Weathered and wintry woodlands whisper in the wind.

   fields: Fuzzy fog hangs over the frozen fields.

   snow: Silver-white snow slips through the air.

Something Told the Wild Geese
Page 45

1. A—fall
2. B—The fields are golden.
3. A—warned
4. B—The trees are heavy with ripe fruit.
5. D—the signs of nature

Page 46

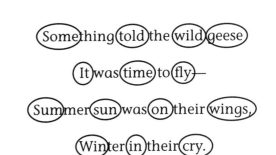

Haiku Collection
Page 50

1. B—They tell about a simple detail in everyday life.
2. C—He is wearing new clothes.
3. D—seventeen
4. D—is the same as the number of syllables
5. B—The men are dizzy from dancing.

Page 51

1. **Worm**

   At / night, / qui/et/ly, (5)

   A / worm / un/der / the / moon/light (7)

   Digs / in/to / a / nut. (5)

   Moon Dance

   Men / dance / round / and / round. (5)

   The / moon / high / a/bove / their / heads (7)

   Is /a/bout / to / fall. (5)

2. Poems will vary.

Tanka Collection
Page 54

1. D—a life full of sadness and worry
2. C—eats away the land
3. B—chases the mouse
4. D—coral reefs
5. A—carelessly

Page 55

1. a. The first line is five syllables.

   b. The second line is seven syllables.

   c. The third line is five syllables.

   d. The fourth line is seven syllables.

   e. The fifth line is seven syllables.

2. Answers will vary. Examples: Absolutely still; Not moving a bit; Quiet as can be

3. Answers will vary. Examples: The cat waits and licks her lips; Waiting for her morning meal

4. Quiet as can be
Waiting for her morning meal
The cat spies a mouse
And thinks to herself: "Aha!
It must be time for breakfast."

5. Poems will vary.

Cinquain Collection
Page 58
1. D—raindrops and gems
2. C—flames of fire
3. D—Raindrops are beautiful, but you can't hold them in your hand.
4. B—brilliantly
5. C—disappear without a trace

Page 59
1. Metaphor—Raindrops are precious gems.
   Simile—The rose's stem is like an arch.
   Metaphor—Trees blaze briefly.
   Simile—Their leaves are like flames of fire.
   Simile—Snowflakes fly like butterflies.
   Metaphor—Snow brushes the trees with
                    its wings.

2. Answers will vary. Examples could include:
   clouds—pillow
   wind—breath
   dry leaves—crumpled paper
   bare tree—skeleton
   stars at night—millions of candles
   line of ants—traffic jam

3. Answers will vary.

Acrostics
Page 62
1. D—the sights, sounds, and tastes of the Caribbean
2. C—The sea is a beautiful green color.
3. C—piñatas
4. B—the play of light on water
5. A—a mirror

Page 63
1. Coral, Anancy, Reggae, Ice, Breadfruit, Blue, Emerald, At, Night

   Slip, Under, Now, Bring, Each, As, Mirror

2. Answers will vary, but should include words that begin with the initial letter of each line and relate to the subject spelled out in the acrostic:

M moon, month
O outer space
O orbit
N new moon
L light
I investigate, important
G galaxy, glimmer
H half moon, high tide
T tilt, tide

A American Indian, Anchorage, Alaska
M mixed heritage, Missouri, Montana
E eagle
R regions, rights, Rhode Island
I individual, Idaho
C Capitol, Constitution, Congress
A Alabama, Arizona

3. Poems will vary.

Concrete Poetry
Page 66
1. D—There's always a piece that hangs off the fork.
2. C—Follow the dangling strands to their ends.
3. A—spaghetti
4. B—frustrated
5. D—a bad mood

Page 67
1. Answers will vary. Examples: tizz—upset; twizzle—twist and turn.
2. Answers will vary. Examples:
   a baby ant: antlet
   the milk and cereal left at the bottom of a bowl: splashover
   an embarrassing mistake: fuddle
   shoelaces that can't be untied: whopperknot
3. Answers will vary. Examples: cloud, falling leaves, roller coaster, candle flame, waterfall, full moon.
4. Responses will vary.

Songs of the First Nations
Page 71
1. D—the tradition of honoring ancestors through the generations
2. B—older members of the community
3. B—a young person
4. A—a spirit
5. D—had great respect for the dead

Page 72

1. _c_ great deeds
   _e_ I will be honored
   _d_ in ancient times
   _f_ old men
   _b_ showing gratitude
   _a_ two wandering spirits

2. Answers will vary. An example might be:

   When I hear the old ones
   Speaking of warriors and wise ones
   From days of old,
   When I listen to tales
   Of the noble ancients
   I know in my heart
   I, too, can strive to be like them.

I Hear, I Hear
Page 75

1. C—the Tarahumara and their way of life
2. B—planting wheat
3. A—They rely on farming for food.
4. D—music
5. B—repetition and rhythm

Page 76

1. a. beating
   b. cooking
   c. farming
   d. herding
   e. hoeing
   f. patting
   g. planting
   h. playing
   i. running
   j. singing

2. Answers will vary. Examples:
   a. hoeing cornfields thunk, thunk
   b. patting tortillas pat, pat
   c. herding goats beeh, beeh
   d. running barefoot pitter-pat, pitter-pat
   e. drumming boom-ah-bahm-boom

3. Answers will vary.
4. Answers will vary.

Waltzing Matilda
Page 79

1. C—by the side of a stream
2. B—put it in a bag
3. C—The swagman jumped into the billabong.
4. D—because he was caught stealing
5. A—why the billabong is haunted

Page 80

Illustrations will vary. Labels should correspond to definitions on page 77.

Sampan
Page 83

1. C—describes the sights and sounds from a boat
2. B—sails on a sampan
3. D—tremble and flicker
4. A—tap tap
5. B—waves, fish, river

Page 84

1. a. tap tap
   b. lap lap
   c. clap clap
   d. flap flap
2. a. achoo
   b. splat
   c. hiss
   d. pitter-pat
   e. buzz
   f. whoosh
3. Answers will vary.

Limerick Collection
Page 88

1. B—had grass all over his body
2. B—teach or to play the flute
3. A—a flue
4. D—Let's get out of here as quickly as we can.
5. C—They flew through a hole.

Page 89

1. Answers will vary, but should be similar to these:

   a. **The first poem** is about a farmer who swallowed six packets of seeds. After awhile, he was covered with grass. He couldn't sit down because of the weeds in the grass.

   b. **The second poem** is about two students studying the flute. They asked their tutor if it was easier for him to play the flute himself or to teach others how to play it.

   c. **The third poem** is about a fly and flea. They were caught in a flue. They started to panic, but then they flew through a hole in the chimney.

2. a. tutor
   b. toot
   c. fly
   d. flea
   e. flee
   f. flaw
   g. flue

Calico Pie
Page 93

1. D—Everybody has gone away.
2. A—fish
3. B—mice drinking tea
4. C—insects
5. D—doesn't make very much sense

Page 94

1. a. around—bound, ground
   b. ban—ran
   c. bee—me, sea, tea, tree
   d. blue—flew, Tilly-loo
   e. come—drum
   f. cup—up, flup
   g. fly—pie
   h. hat—sprat, Willeby-Wat
   i. jam—swam

2. Answers will vary. Examples could be:

   calico pie=a pie with bright designs on it

   syllabub sea=a sea made out of jelly

   Flippety flup=a slurping sound

   Tilly-loo=the sound a bird makes

   Willeby-Wat=a small fish like sole and sprat

The Platypus
Page 97

1. B—how hard it is to classify the platypus
2. D—a mammal
3. C—puzzled
4. D—They didn't know how to categorize the platypus.
5. C—It doesn't make any sense.

Page 98

1.

Mammals	Birds	Fish
cat	duck	goldfish
elephant	eagle	salmon
horse	goose	shark
monkey	hummingbird	trout
tiger	owl	tuna

2. Answers will vary.

The Walrus and the Carpenter
Page 102

1. A—on a beach
2. B—angrily
3. C—was shining in the middle of the night
4. D—there was so much sand on the beach
5. B—make people laugh

Page 103

1. Answers will vary.
2. The sea was wet.

   The sands were dry.

   The sky was clear because there weren't any clouds.

   No birds were flying because there were no birds to fly.

3. If seven maids swept the beach for seven years, could they sweep away all the sand on the beach?

The Bold Pedlar and Robin Hood
Page 109

1. A—on a country road
2. D—suits and strings made out of silk
3. C—rob the Pedlar of his belongings
4. B—They all went to a tavern.
5. A—were related

Page 110

Answers will vary, but should correspond to this:

Beginning
The Pedlar was traveling down a country road and he came upon Robin Hood and Little John. Robin Hood asked the Pedlar what he had in the bag, and he told him that he had some silk. Robin Hood asked for the silk, and the Pedlar refused to give it to him.

Middle
The Pedlar fought with Little John until Little John got tired out. Then Robin Hood took over. He got tired, too. He wondered who the Pedlar was, so he asked him. They figured out that they were cousins.

End
Robin Hood and the Pedlar stopped fighting and went to a tavern where they all ate and drank as friends.

Hiawatha's Childhood
Page 116
1. C—about the world of nature
2. D—a daughter of the moon
3. A—a baby owl
4. B—fire-fly, owl, beaver
5. D—was more than an ordinary human being

Page 117

He was born on the shore of a lake. Nearby was a dark forest.

She sang him lullabies and rocked him to sleep.

She taught him about the stars and spirits of the night.

He heard the sound of wind in the trees and lapping water.

He saw a fire-fly, and asked it to light up the wigwam.

She said that a warrior threw his grandmother up against the moon, and that we can still see her shadow there today.

She said that all flowers blossom in heaven when they die on earth.

She said that they were scolding each other.

He decided to learn the language of birds and all the other animals.

A Visit from St. Nicholas
Page 122
1. C—a father who catches a glimpse of St. Nicholas
2. D—in the middle of the night
3. B—reindeer
4. C—filled the stockings
5. B—went to another house

Page 123
1. _1_ Everybody goes to bed.

   _2_ Papa hears a loud noise outside.

   _3_ The reindeer land on the roof.

   _4_ St. Nicholas comes down the chimney.

   _5_ Papa watches St. Nick fill the stockings.

   _6_ After he goes back up the chimney, St. Nick drives away on his sleigh.

2. a. St. Nick's nose was as red as a cherry.

   b. His cheeks were like roses.

   c. His mouth was like a bow.

   d. Smoke circled his head like a wreath.

   e. The beard of his chin was as white as snow.

   f. When he laughed, his belly shook like a bowl full of jelly.

3. Answers will vary. Possible answers include:

   a. The night was as dark as coal.

   b. The stars twinkled like candles.

   c. Something made a noise that sounded like hooves on the roof.

   d. St. Nick came down the chimney as quiet as a mouse.

   e. His helpers were as tiny as dolls.

   f. They climbed the Christmas tree like squirrels.

Read and Understand Poetry • EMC 3324 • ©2005 by Evan-Moor Corp.